STRATEGY ACTIVATION CANVAS

First published 2024
by Routledge
4 Park Square, Milton Park, Abingdon, Oxon OX14 4RN

and by Routledge
605 Third Avenue, New York, NY 10158

Routledge is an imprint of the Taylor & Francis Group, an informa business

British Library Cataloguing-in-Publication Data
A catalogue record for this book is available from the British Library

Library of Congress Cataloging-in-Publication Data
Names: Thiessen, Ansgar, author. | Wreschniok, Robert, author. | Svetov, Mark, 1951- translator. Title: Strategy activation canvas / Ansgar Thiessen & Robert Wreschniok. Other titles: Playbook Strategie-Aktivierung. English Description: Abingdon, Oxon ; New York, NY : Routledge, 2024. | Translation of: Playbook Strategie-Aktivierung : Das Standardwerk für Strategen, Organisationsentwickler, Führungskräfte und Entscheider der neuen Generation. | Includes bibliographical references. Identifiers: LCCN 2023028183 (print) | LCCN 2023028184 (ebook) | ISBN 9781032472263 (hardback) | ISBN 9781003388791 (ebook) Subjects: LCSH: Leadership. | Organizational change. Classification: LCC HD57.7 .T46525 2024 (print) | LCC HD57.7 (ebook) | DDC 658.4/092--dc23/eng/20230829 LC record available at https://lccn.loc.gov/2023028183 LC ebook record available at https://lccn.loc.gov/2023028184

ISBN: 978-1-032-47226-3 (hbk)
ISBN: 978-1-003-38879-1 (ebk)

DOI: 10.4324/9781003388791

Typeset in Museo Slab and Museo Sans by
TATIN Institute GmbH, Munich, Germany

Translation: Marc Svetov, www.transatlantichabit.com
Designed cover image: Jan Reisser Illustrator, Munich, Germany
Layout cover image: TATIN Institute GmbH, Munich, Germany

Publisher's note: This book has been prepared from camera-ready copy provided by the authors.

STRATEGY ACTIVATION
CANVAS

The new standard for acceleration strategies.
For decision-makers and leaders of a new generation.

Ansgar Thiessen & Robert Wreschniok

Routledge
Taylor & Francis Group

LONDON AND NEW YORK

FOREWORD BY

BARBARA KELLERMAN

HARVARD KENNEDY SCHOOL

With inspiring practical examples from Allianz, Baloise, E.ON, Hamburg Commercial Bank, Microsoft, NORD/LB, Swisscom and Swiss Re.

Table of Contents

The fields of impact of the Strategy Activation Canvas

The genius of the person who knows is worthless without the genius of the person who understands.

Pablo Picasso

Foreword
Followers to the front

The Strategy Activation Canvas comes at a right time — in fact, it's a management handbook which is almost overdue. For a long time, the emphasis on how to develop societies, industries, corporations or teams has been put on leaders and their system of bringing change to people. This playbook takes a refreshingly different approach, proclaiming an inclusion, a participation, in short the activation of humans in order to unleash the belief in a common goal, shaping a bright future together. This change of perspective — from leaders to followers — is at the heart of modern management literature indeed. Let me explain why.

Barbara Kellerman
Harvard Kennedy School

Past

The history of followership — as theory, as practice — is not pretty. For most of human history the interest has been in leaders, not followers. Nor has this changed during the heyday of what I call the 'leadership industry,' the last forty years or so during which have mushroomed countless leadership centers, programs, courses, workshops, books, articles, webinars, videos, conferences, consultants and coaches that claim to teach people, usually for money, how to lead.

There have been a few exceptions to this general rule, when the emphasis shifted from leaders to followers, such as, for example, in the 1950s and '60s when social scientists sought to explain what happened in Germany during the Nazi period not just by looking at the leadership class but at the citizenry more generally. Still, in recent decades the leadership industry has been fixated on the person(s) at the top while remaining largely oblivious to those in the middle and at the bottom.

Why this should be so has never been completely clear. After all, it is widely agreed that leadership is a relationship which requires, at a minimum, a leader and one follower. Moreover, the first is dependent, entirely, on the second.

There can be no leadership without followership, no leader without a single follower, which makes the omission of followers from the leadership industry that much more puzzling. But, as indicated, the leadership industry is a money maker. This suggests that part of the problem is incentive. We leadership 'experts' typically get paid for teaching people how to lead. We do not get paid – though we should – for teaching people how to follow.

Another part of the problem is semantic. The word itself – 'follower' – implies weakness and passivity. Its counterpart – 'leader' – suggests just the opposite. Strength, success, action and activity, and control. Yet if we take the time to define the word, 'follower,' the problem melts away. I have found this definition to be the most useful: Followers are subordinates who have less power, authority, and influence than do their superiors, and who therefore usually, but not invariably, fall into line.

Defining followers this way has two obvious advantages. The first is clarity – followers are defined by rank, not behavior. The second is it makes it apparent that followers – those lower on the hierarchy of power, authority, and influence – do not necessarily follow. They usually follow, but they do not always.

Present

The fact that followers as I define them do not necessarily follow is important. For people in the present feel freer than they did in the past to disregard or even disobey people in positions of authority. Which is why leaders in recent decades have become weaker and followers stronger. Authority, which is associated with position, has diminished both in status and importance. Therefore, being in a higher position grants neither the respect that it once did, nor the trust.

This shift does not, obviously, apply in the same way to autocracies. In fact, in the last ten years most autocrats have become more authoritarian, not less, precisely in response to the point that I make. They recognize full well that unless they are more controlling now than they used to be – Turkey's President Recep Tayyip Erdoğan, and China's President Xi Jinping are examples – they will be in greater danger now of losing control than they would have been.

> Authority, which is associated with position, has diminished both in status and importance.

In liberal democracies in contrast – from the United States to the United Kingdom, from Chile to Ecuador to Bolivia – leaders have been weakened and followers strengthened. This shift applies as much to the private sector as to the public one. Consider this metric: The number of chief executive officers who left their posts in 2019 was the highest in the almost two decades since the tracking firm Challenger started counting.

Said Challenger's head: 'The number of chief executives who announced their departures in 2019 was staggering.' So, why is it that business leaders are leaving their posts in droves? While the reasons are various, what I am suggesting is that highest on the list is followers – boards, clients, customers, suppliers, media, employees, the public – who have made the jobs of CEOs that much more difficult. That much more stressful, that much less rewarding in every way other than financially. CEOs remain obviously, by definition, in positions of authority. But equally obviously their positions of authority confer less power and less influence than they used to.

What this makes clear is that the old ways of looking at leadership have become antiquated and inadequate. To look at leadership only through the lens of the leader will no longer suffice. Instead, better now to see leadership as a system. The leadership system has three parts, each of which is equally important, and each of which impinges equally on the other two. The first part is the leader, the second is the follower, and the third is the context within which both leaders and followers necessarily are located.

Never underestimate the significance of context.

In fact, just as the importance of the follower must never be underestimated, especially not now, in the third decade of the 21st century, so the importance of the context must never be underestimated either. Changes in culture and technology particularly have changed forever the balance of power and influence between leaders and followers – unless coercion is part of the equation.

Future

I am an American. So far be it from me to underestimate the importance of the leader. Having lived for four years in a country led by President Donald Trump was a vivid reminder if any were needed that leaders do matter. But, to understand the phenomenon that was Trump he cannot be looked at in isolation. He must be seen in tandem with his followers. And he must be seen within the context that is the United States of America in the here and now.

Trump was a disrupter, no doubt. But he could not possibly have disrupted without the support of, or at least the complicity of followers that ranged from ordinary Americans, specifically his dedicated and devoted base, to Senate Republicans, who nearly in their entirety remained for the duration of his presidency slavishly loyal. Similarly, this same man would never have been tolerated by his Republican peers even a decade earlier. The United States has, in short, changed. The political landscape, the political culture, was different in 2016 from what it was in 2006.

America had become more fiercely divided. Income inequity was that much more extreme. The collective conversation was harsher and coarser. And the technologies that were fledgling a decade previous had become that much more ubiquitous and, sometimes, insidious.

There are reasons why liberal democracies – and the individuals and institutions that populate them – are finding leadership and management more difficult now than before. No accident, for example, that in the last ten years the number of democracies around the world has significantly decreased, while the number of autocracies has significantly increased. As Freedom House recently put it with unsettling economy and accuracy, 'pluralism and democracy' are everywhere 'under assault.'

So, attention must be paid. It must be paid to leaders, and to followers, and to the various context within which they are situated. For the purposes of this essay though a concluding cautionary note: If you are a leader, better pay attention not only to yourself, but to your followers.

To your subordinates, your employees, your constituents, even to your peers. For only by paying less attention to yourself and more to those around you will you be able to navigate leadership in the twenty-first century successfully. Contexts are changing. Followers are changing. Which is why leaders who lead in the present as they did in the past do so at their peril.

If you share this idea of followership and if you want to shape your organisation towards a social movements, which activates its strategy broad scale, then the Strategy Activation Canvas must find its place in your bookshelf alongside central pieces of management literature.

Prof. Barbara Kellerman
Cambridge (Massachusetts), June 2023

Foreword
On strategies and their activation

There has been a fundamental change for how business strategies are developed and brought to life: From the formulation of analytical, oftentimes quite intricate concept papers, accessible only to a few; toward a target vision that has been jointly developed, is based on the true realities of the company and is forward-looking and inspiring.

Ansgar Thiessen
Global Head of Operational
Excellence, Swiss Re Corporate
Solutions

And also the way companies put strategies into action is changing accordingly: Up to now, strategies frequently consisted largely or mainly of a concept paper with strong content, containing many facts, logical arguments, supported by studies and analyses (e.g. the analyses of investment bankers or assessments by strategy consultants). This is not wrong in itself. Strategies are undoubtedly concerned with the path a company wants to take in order to reach a specific and defined target vision of the future. Which is ultimately measured by business success, financial indicators and economic value.

But what if this path, this direction to be taken, is reserved to only an exclusive group? If strategies are solely understood by a few people since they are worded in a special, highly abstract language? Or what if strategies are reduced to hollow phrases when communicated? (Who, for instance, would be opposed to a strategy committed to 'digitization', a 'heightened customer focus' or 'accelerated innovation cycles'?) Although these and similar words convey meaning, the span of interpretation is so wide that in many cases many on the workforce and in middle management have a hard time reconciling the postulated assumptions and objectives with the corporate reality they perceive and specifically implement them. It is even harder for teams and employees to relate their own work to these goals.

Robert Wreschniok
CEO, TATIN Institute for
Strategy Activation

The result: Strategies remain nothing more than brilliant papers for a small group of insiders and then must be interpreted by middle management, leading to a wide range of results, from successful to less successful.

Strategies as a key to business development

This Strategy Activation Canvas is designed as a management handbook for strategists, organizational developers and leaders of a new generation. It is deliberately not a plea for distilling strategy development in companies so it ends up evaporating – on the contrary. Strategy is and will remain the key to moving away from a purely evolutionary corporate development and achieving new objectives more rapidly and with greater precision, underpinned by financial targets and control mechanisms[1]. The task is to prevent that the path, from developing a strategy to achieving it, will not branch out completely or even be disrupted. And this is not a theoretical issue. Empirical studies and findings from many years of working with management boards demonstrate:

- seven out of ten strategic projects or initiatives fall short of expectations (cf. Bund Deutscher Unternehmensberater 2015); or

- around 60% of managers are unable to explain their own strategy compellingly to a colleague (cf. Monster 2016).

- The result is that the gap between strategic ambition and implementation in the real-world company environment is alarmingly wide (cf. McKinsey 2018).

All this need not be. Companies have come to realize: The activation of strategies works best if executives succeed in transforming abstract ideas into tangible, specific goals and getting their teams excited about them. A strategy thrives on people believing in it and, above all, people understanding how they can make a personal contribution to the common success. For these companies, the value of a strategy is not measured alone by revenue goals but also by the number of followers they can gather for these goals. The more stakeholders they can convince that the strategy will work, the more valuable it will become.

> The more stakeholders they can convince that the strategy will work, the more valuable it will become.

The Strategy Activation Canvas summarizes what we've experienced during our working together with large corporations and global corporations. It is complemented by discourses and dialogs from the 'Future of Leadership Initiative,' a series of talks with experienced executives and academics on the subject of corporate leadership and people management. The conceptual framework, the Strategy Activation Canvas, which we are introducing in this play-book, is augmented by numerous examples from new-generation leaders who have made a name for themselves in the field of organizational development.

We would like to express our gratitude to our co-authors Kaja Wilkniss, Adrian Bucher, Jean-Philippe Courtois, Beat Knechtli, Frank Meyer, Sabine Pudsack, Oliver Stein, Ulrich Tennie and Tony White, who showcase case studies that make strategy activation visible in an impressive way.

The Strategy Activation Canvas doesn't claim to be exhaustive. On the contrary, it is designed for being absolutely compatible with powerful and proven mechanisms that many executives already apply to their strategy work today. The book is a framework, a source of ideas and a logic for complementing existing strategy work in a way that's sensible and adds value.

We hope reading this book will give you joy and, most importantly, inspiration – and above all fresh ideas for strategy work that will fundamentally change your own company or environment, so you will create your future actively and with the greatest possible creation of value.

Ansgar Thiessen & Robert Wreschniok
Zurich & Munich, June 2023

You don't have to be great to start but you have to start to be great.

Zig Ziglar

Figure 1: Section of a Big Picture of the vision of generation Y on the future of the world, TATIN Institute 2023

INTRODUCTION

Why is the global proportion of employees who are engaged in their work so low?

There are many potential reasons — but resistance to change is a common underlying theme.

Introduction
Business transformation as a social movement

'Something's going awry in today's organizations.' In his book 'Reinventing Organization' (cf. Laloux 2016), Frederic Laloux describes a reality that we have frequently discovered when working with companies: An overwhelming quantity of goals and conflicting goals; frustration with nonsensical policies and sensitivities; a decline in commitment; or even a lethargic attitude towards change initiatives. And above all a system of 'command and control,' i.e. constantly working for a supervisor or a steering committee. All this in an environment of hundreds of emails, meetings or PowerPoint presentations, prereads, action logs and calls for a vote.

Exaggerated? Not at all, as global studies show, such as that of Gallup ('State of the Global Workplace' 2017). These studies found that large sections of the workforce were dissatisfied and there was a lack of inspiration on the part of middle management. With devastating consequences. According to Gallup, stagnating commitment impacts commercial success, which is reflected on the balance sheet (cf. Gallup, 2017). Laloux responds to these grievances and impressively describes the evolution from conformist and performance-oriented organizations still predominant today toward pluralistic and even evolutionary philosophies for the organization of work (not of people).

At the core of this evolution is understanding organizations as living systems, as social movements of people, who will unfold their full potential if they can decide freely while the system nonetheless adheres together as a whole. This is facilitated by distributed authority, collective intelligence, playing a part in the work and being guided by a common destiny, instead of predicting a future and following this prediction.

Utopia?

Again: Not quite. There have been impressive examples of companies that practice these forms of organization and show how people can collaborate in a way that creates meaning and value (cf. Laloux 2016).

Aaron Dignan argues in a similar way when he describes the 'Brave New Work' (2019) – well-nigh a logical continuation of Laloux's work. Dignan begins with the metaphor of traffic lights and roundabouts: While traffic lights clearly regulate traffic and completely relieve road users of the need to think, roundabouts are the exact opposite: The traffic remains in flux but demands full commitment and decision-making from road users.

What's astounding: The number of accidents at traffic lights is significantly higher, and the traffic flows a lot better at roundabouts than at traffic lights. Dignan argues that companies today simply have the wrong operating system, see Chapter  Baloise Group: Emotions, people and networks – not processes and hierarchies: Brilliant minds and creative ideas are either nipped in the bud by stringent rules and organizational boundaries or lose their effectiveness in the medium term.

So Dignan advocates the change from 'Control Inc.' to 'Emergent Inc.,' i.e. from the prototype of command and control to organizations as living organisms. What's special about his argumentation: Dignan applies the idea to the process of change, i.e. change as an emergent learning process that puts people in the center, involves them completely and is continuously renegotiated.

The COVID-19 crisis of 2020 brought forth something interesting: It has pushed many of us out of our office spaces. 'New Work' is thus something like a complementary ideology of those conformist organizational systems. Because all of a sudden it became necessary to collaborate at a distance, asynchronously, with working hours based on trust and the measurement of results – a reality that keeps organizational developers, HR managers and executives quite busy at the moment. Habitual mechanisms have lost their effectiveness almost overnight. What's important now is to design new ones in a meaningful way.

The work of Otto Scharmer, 'From Ego-System to Eco-System Economies' (cf. Scharmer 2013) seems almost prophetic, because he shows – likewise on the basis of a systemic conception of man – that organizational development needs to respond to a future that is no longer clearly predictable.

Similar to Laloux and Dignan, Scharmer underscores: The prevailing management reality is subject to an economic imperative and manifests something that he outlines as the ego-system. This is opposed by a future that is networked, evolutionary, holistic, sometimes irrational (cf. the work of Nobel Prize winner Daniel Kahnemann), i.e. subject to the laws of an eco-system. Overcoming habitual forms of management is one of the top challenges in organizational development and thus for leaders in companies.

Kim & Mauborgne showed many years ago what this means for companies during strategy development with their idea of a 'Blue Ocean Strategy' (cf. Kim et al. 2005). Not the optimization of a corporate strategy in rigid thought patterns, i.e. existing markets, known systems, servicing existing needs, etc., accelerates corporate success but one that sees and considers the overall system. Only when you have a systemic perspective on the prevailing corporate reality can you make a conscious strategic decision on where you want to break through this reality, thus differentiating

How to respond to the current waves of disruptive change from a deep place that connects us to the emerging future rather than by reacting against the patterns of the past, which usually means perpetuating them.

Otto Scharmer: From ego-system to eco-system economies.

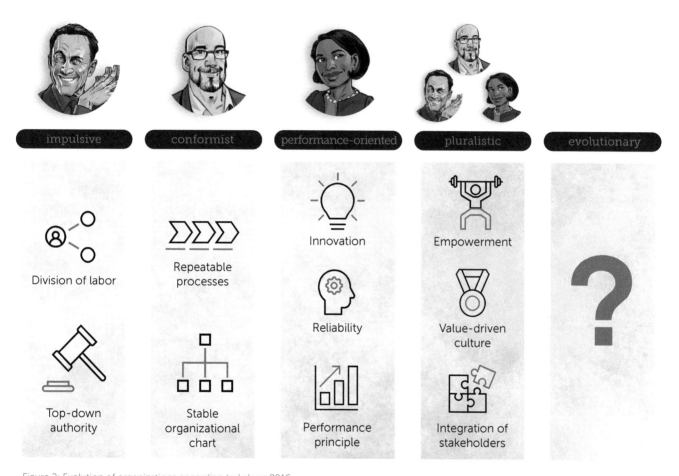

impulsive	conformist	performance-oriented	pluralistic	evolutionary
Division of labor	Repeatable processes	Innovation	Empowerment	?
Top-down authority	Stable organizational chart	Reliability	Value-driven culture	
		Performance principle	Integration of stakeholders	

Figure 2: Evolution of organizations according to Laloux 2016

yourself. According to Kim & Mauborgne, this means getting from the 'red ocean' into the 'blue ocean,' with the result that competition ultimately becomes irrelevant.

In one fell swoop 'Nine Lies about Work' by Marcus Buckingham and Ashley Goodall (cf. Buckingham et al. 2019) does away with prevalent assumptions in major companies. The authors show, for instance, how companies love to boast that people stay with them due to their wonderful culture. In reality, there are as many reasons as there are employees for why people remain loyal to a company. Or the assumption that the best plan, the best strategy will win. Ultimately, plans only help to identify a problem – not to resolve it.

This means that solutions are not found in plans but in the creativity of those who solve problems. Another die-hard assumption is that setting goals and breaking them down into steps helps to create alignment. But for goals to be meaningful and motivating, the opposite is true: They must be thought through and formulated from within by the employees themselves. Employees are perfectly capable of setting their own goals in the interest of the company. In short, Buckingham and Goodall show that prevailing assumptions and mechanisms such as targets, the alleged importance of feedback, plans or employee potential must at least be questioned (cf. Buckingham et al. 2029).

> This means that solutions are not found in plans but in the creativity of those who solve problems.

What we want to say: With this playbook, we want to re-think and supplement the works that have defined change literature for a long time and that have evolved from Kotter's school of thought (cf. John P. Kotter, 2007), in which transformations and strategy implementations in a company are built like a second 'operating system.' Companies in our understanding are social movements – and so are any changes in

Figure 3: The change trap. Rotating around yourself doesn't bring you forward, TATIN Institute 2023

them. With the Strategy Activation Canvas, we show that change doesn't need to be a preconceived top-down future, which is then controlled by means of predictable and wisely orchestrated mechanisms. Instead, we want to reinforce the view that change must be directed inwardly by directing change going forward.

With this we are challenging the narrow idea of 'I'll tell you how you have to change' and countering it with: 'This is the common idea, and this is how we could experience it – what can your skills, networks and your experience contribute?' In short: 'How can we get involved as people to shape (across functions) our common destiny?'

Strategy Activation Canvas

The Strategy Activation Canvas is committed to provide a management approach that addresses this new business reality. It seeks to make tools available to executives to help them shape powerful strategies using the dynamics of social systems in an ever-changing future. It supplements existing systems of developing strategies and business models (see e.g. Osterwalder & Pigneur: 'Business Model Canvas' 2011), i.e. it activates (and doesn't define) existing strategies.

Thus it nicely links to strategy development – and bridges to management literature on change through complementing it significantly: The Canvas proclaims an approach in which people in organizations not only experience strategies but become the driving force behind the strategy. The approach showcased in this book creates an entrepreneurial vitality that no roadshow, town-hall meeting and other known change/communication mechanisms are anywhere near to achieving. The aim is clear: Visualizing a strategy and making it tangible.

The Canvas proclaims an approach in which people in organizations not only experience strategies but become the driving force behind the strategy.

Introduction
Social dynamics that prevent strategy implementation

When we started to address the subject of strategy activation, we were more or less alone. We had insight into many companies and C-suites, yet we were never quite satisfied with the answers we got to questions of why teams, business units, segments, functions or entire companies have such a hard time in bringing strategies to life, beyond the boardroom. The more we looked into the dynamics of social movements and organizational forms, the more often we came across organizations that showed resoundingly how it's done: To induce enthusiasm in people in their thousands for a new path, completely outside the usual management theory (a global example is shown in Chapter ➡ Microsoft: Help shaping a new era – activating Microsoft's strategic core worldwide). What then is the difference between these two types of organizations – those that have such a hard time and those that are so good at it?

Initially, we were surprised – in 2017 around EUR 7.7 billion was spent on strategy consultancy (cf. Bundesverband Deutscher Unternehmensberater [German Association of Management Consultants], 2018). Globally, the figure is as much as $160 billion – and the market is seen as definitely expanding (cf. Statista Research 2021). The need for advice in the strategy development phase and support in strategy implementation seems enormous. And with eroding markets, new technologies coming at us like crazy, markets that can hardly be demarcated and blurred customer segments, etc., it is understandable. What's even more surprising is that around 70% of strategy projects don't meet expectations or meet them to a very limited extent. In fact, 67% miss the target completely. No wonder then that only 14% of CEOs rate their company as effective when it comes to implementing new strategies (see Ewenstein, Smith & Sologar 2015 as well as Ernst & Young 2019). Now that's truly astounding. Strategies are fleshed out, which, as we've seen, are often quite ingenious and well-thought-out, making total sense and reading like a blueprint for the future. And then they grind to a halt in just those places where they should happen or, at a minimum, don't deliver the hoped-for result. Our answer to the question of why strategy activation is so important is that of social dynamics. The strategies themselves are not to blame nor the analyses and arguments that led to them but....

- a management team that doesn't know the strategy or knows only parts/snippets of it....

- and therefore doesn't understand the Big Picture and its context.

- employees who are primarily concerned with optimizing their own position, their own team (including in transformation situations).

- a dominant mindset of 'This won't work because...' or

- employees who mentally drop out as soon as they hear the word 'change' and help only superficially with the project.

This sums up our observations and reflections from decades of consulting. Let's add numbers to this: What actually are measurable 'social dynamics' that stand in the way of a successful activation? We summed up four gaps, i.e. differences between aspirations and reality, to capture what's preventing activation.

Alignment Gap

Around two-thirds of all managers can't explain their own business strategy precisely (see Bradley, Hirt & Smit 2018). In their book 'Strategy Beyond the Hockey Stick,' Bradley, Hirt & Smit elucidate the dilemma in which the management of major corporations frequently find themselves: If your own management team cannot clearly articulate what path the company is meant to take, how can enthusiasm be induced in business units, teams and individual employees?

If one-third of all the executives don't even have any awareness of what something new means, then one-third of the top executives of an enterprise are comfortable navigating within the status quo.

The alignment gap thus defines the gap between strategy understanding within the management team and between the management team and employees.

Focus Gap

The second gap we see is a lack of context and of focus. Companies launch one initiative after another – they're all important, they all run more or less in tandem with one another. And the fact that companies are typically organized in functional units with experts (about 78%) fosters a certain expert view of problems (see Bradley, Hirt & Smit 2018)[2]. This means that market units look at the future from the perspective of growth; operations from that of processes required for growth; IT from the perspective of systems; HR from that of skills and resources, etc.

If they look at all! Usually they are too busy maintaining the status quo. Simply due to their organizational structure, many companies struggle to grasp and deal with topics holistically and across functions and departments. A 'focus' on too many priorities inevitably stifles the power to make a strategy successful (cf. Anand & Barsoux 2017). At the same time, there is a lack of knowledge of how all the initiatives are ultimately connected. The focus gap thus defines the gap between a clearly delineated North Star and the reality of the associated projects and initiatives in daily work.

Commitment Gap

77% of companies[3] say they have in parts a culture of 'destructive criticism' (cf. Hays 2015/2016). Conversely, the experts on corporate culture from Human Synergistics show in a study that included 740 Australian and New Zealand companies that organizations with a constructive culture attain 64% higher employee motivation than their peers, a 32% higher level of satisfaction, 24% better collaboration and an impressive 86% better collaboration between functional silos. Such organizations are also seen as 54% more capable of adapting to changing external circumstances (cf. 'Organisational Culture: Beyond Employee Engagement', without author). In the same study, the experts show for the aforementioned companies that far more than one-half of the examined enterprises in total are below the global average of those companies that were measured in terms of corporate culture in the global survey database.

In short: A destructive culture makes it difficult for employees to engage in shaping a new target vision. The commitment gap thus defines the gap between the necessary commitment and the reality in the company in terms of behavior and culture.

Action Gap

80% of employees in companies have personal or factual reservations when it comes to change. 15% even actively resist (cf. Mohr, Woehe & Diebold 1998). While the plan to lead a company into the future still sounds plausible and is welcomed, this quickly fizzles out when it comes to adapting one's own actions to the plan.

We see one of the reasons for this in the predominant opinion that changes à la Kotter must always be accompanied by a change organization (cf. Kotter 2018 and Lewin 1947). In reality, such an organization is not always necessary or is necessary only in parts. The deliberate realignment of ongoing projects and initiatives alone can make employees act together. And yet: In many companies, change is rejected as annoying, unnecessary and a distraction from day-to-day business – and in terms of people's own actions as something that hopefully will pass soon so they can get back to business as usual.

Figure 4: Who wants to change according to School for Change Agents 2018

Making use of social dynamics

This is exactly the point at which strategy activation comes in. It can be understood as dealing intelligently with the social dynamics described above.

- By ensuring that all those who are important to a strategy clearly understand it as well as the 'why' behind it;

- by creating a sharp focus, showing context and providing a simple, emotional and visual story;

- by valuing personal experience and strengths so as to make a transparent personal contribution: What is my personal role, my own contribution to the new strategy; as well as

- by making this relevance visible by tangible common strategic goals that are shaped by working on them across teams.

This is strategy activation in a nutshell.

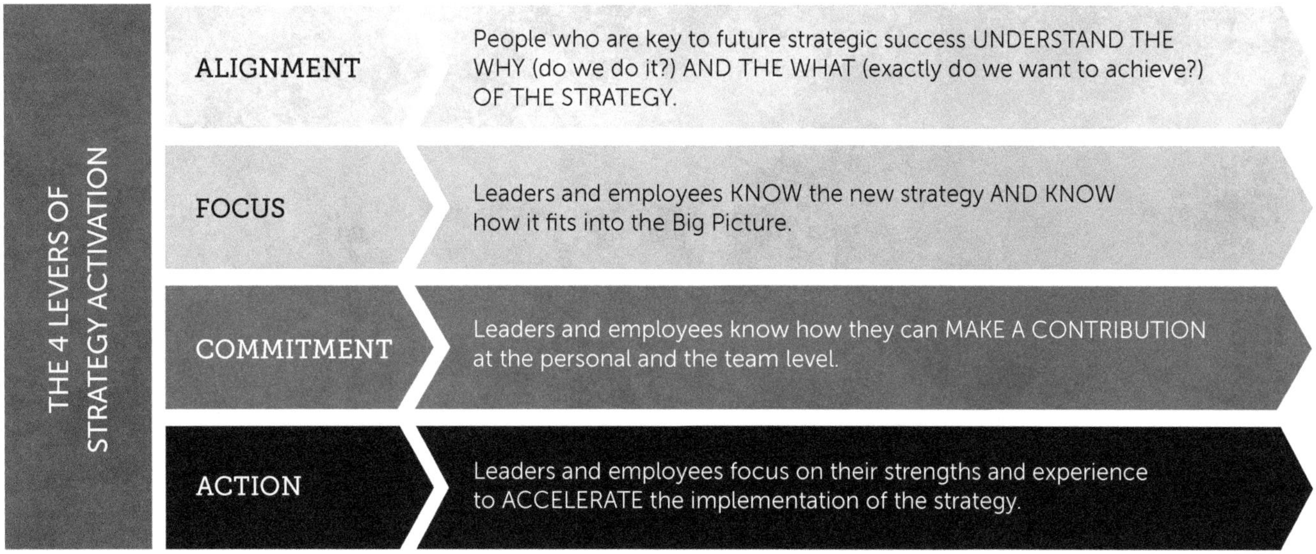

THE 4 LEVERS OF STRATEGY ACTIVATION

ALIGNMENT

People who are key to future strategic success UNDERSTAND THE WHY (do we do it?) AND THE WHAT (exactly do we want to achieve?) OF THE STRATEGY.

FOCUS

Leaders and employees KNOW the new strategy AND KNOW how it fits into the Big Picture.

COMMITMENT

Leaders and employees know how they can MAKE A CONTRIBUTION at the personal and the team level.

ACTION

Leaders and employees focus on their strengths and experience to ACCELERATE the implementation of the strategy.

Figure 5: The four levers of strategy activation, TATIN Institute 2023

Introduction
This book is for ...

You first and foremost. This book was recommended to you, you discovered it by chance, it was a gift or a conscious purchase – no matter, it will transform your ideas about strategy and organizational development. You are holding a book that was written with the active help of leaders, strategists, HR managers and experts in corporate culture, scholars and designers, so you may certainly look forward to many stimulating ideas. This book is particularly for ...

'Players'
Because it is a 'playbook,' a guide for playing and trying out. Deliberately, it has no beginning and end, no course from A to Z. It is a workbook with tried-and-tested mechanisms, with case studies, with modular elements that can be combined and taken apart again. The playbook is intended as a stimulus for debate and for in-depth discussions on your (leadership) team, for questioning and, above all, for breaking up existing working methods. It's a loose manuscript that provides support and can be a guide for systemizing strategy and organizational work. It's also a game board that serves as a reference for individual moves or for the overall goal. Depending on where you and your team are currently moving on the playing field.

Example ➜ Microsoft: Help shaping a new era
Example ➜ Swisscom: Playful, interactive and fun

This book is for all those who shape strategy work with playful ease, who learn from things in the past and integrate them in the future, who try out new things, take risks yet hew to standards, maybe break them consciously and redefine them.

'First followers'

To start with a major transformation, the executive who initiated the whole thing is not the most important person: Instead, it's the so-called 'first follower'. It's important to make this differentiation, because as an executive, owing to your role and position, people see you as someone who shows the way forward. First followers don't have this quality. As organizational developers, we sometime take on both roles: That of an executive who must induce enthusiasm on teams and in large organizations. And that of the organizational developer, who shows leadership teams new ways to shape a transformation. Either way, in the end it's crucial to induce enthusiasm in first followers and with it trigger an epidemic or a social movement.

By the way, this is often the reason why employees who were appointed 'change agents' or 'strategic ambassadors' often fail – they are perceived in their role as executives, not as followers. Winning followers can be actively directed – for one, by means of activation mechanisms (see Chapter ➔ Accelerating strategy and transformation processes); and second, by the setup and management of coalitions and networks (see Chapter ➔ Forming a coalition for change: The movement).

Example ➔ Baloise Group: Emotions, people and networks –
not processes and hierarchies

The Strategy Activation Canvas is for first followers because they are the ones who activate a strategic idea, believe in a strategic momentum and who are able to anchor it in the organization and make it grow.

New generation leaders

In the 'Future of Leadership Initiative,' we had the privilege of working with personalities such as Jimmy Wales, Barbara Kellerman, Muhammad Yunus, Joe Kaeser and Janina Kugel. Through the dialog with these experts, we learned that there actually are leaders in companies who deliberately distance themselves from a form of management described in textbooks or business schools and break new ground; or they supplement established doctrine with new ideas in a meaningful way. They are managers who question established mechanisms and connections and break free from the autopilot of standards and processes.

This book is for these leaders who see strategy work primarily as an organizational task. For leaders who are concerned with market developments and return on investments without neglecting behavior and human needs. Leaders who are capable of questioning and advancing their own role. In the words of Bill Joiner: People who develop from an expert leader who contributes knowledge and experience to problem solving into a politician/networker who is able to forge alliances and pursue goals tactically and then into a 'catalyst,' a coach who keeps himself in the background and helps strong teams and individuals to help themselves (see Joiner 2006).

> This book is for these leaders who see strategy work primarily as an organizational task.

Example ➡ Swiss Re: Activation of the global HR function
           to support the focus on more agility

This book is for leaders who keenly seek new approaches, who have shaped the strategy and organizational work over the last few decades and now want to try out something new.

Transformers

We distinguish between 'change' and 'transformation' in the Strategy Activation Canvas. The crucial difference for us lies in the fact that with 'change' you can always go back to the previous state. A 'transformation' by contrast lifts you into a state that is completely new – a stage of development that cannot be undone. We are familiar with this differentiation from personal development (cf. Loevinger 1976) as well as from the development of organizations: For instance, progressing into new markets with new access mechanisms, new products, new behavior of employees, etc., nearly turns organizations into new enterprises (without throwing the foundations overboard). This playbook is for all those who actively shape the path of transformation – and refrain from 'change,' e.g. in a new operating model that can be reversed if it is not successful.

Strategists

And hence especially for those who have gone through 'classic' strategy schools. Because the book definitely provides ideas that usefully augment the well-known approaches with formats of integration, of crowd sourcing, activation, thus gaining greater acceptance and feasibility for one's own strategy.

A global community

The Strategy Activation Canvas is not the answer to everything. On the contrary, existing activations are happening in numerous companies and teams who are already actively shaping strategies today. To take that into account and learn from one another, we provide the Canvas at www.strategy-activation.com – for trying things out, forming leadership teams, working at the levels of strategy and corporate development.

Introduction
Pictures and figures in this Strategy Activation Canvas

The characters that accompany you in this Strategy Activation Canvas are taken from the strategy activation of the insurance corporation Allianz (#lead), where at a global level more than 18,000 executives worked on the topics of leadership behavior and responsibilities interactively with one another.

They are symbols for activation architectures and constitute the visual complement to the texts of the Strategy Activation Canvas.

Figure 6: Section of a Big Picture on the subject of transformation and how to connect hierarchy and network, TATIN Institute 2023

THE
STRATEGY ACTIVATION
CANVAS

The Strategy Activation Canvas
At a glance

The playbook unfolds its contents along the so-called Strategy Activation Canvas – a framework that links together the main areas of strategy activation. No time to go into details? Then this chapter is just right for you: Here you get a consolidated notion of working with the Strategy Activation Canvas, so you can start right away. The next chapter then dips deeper into the content.

Movement

Who are my first followers? What coalitions do I have to form? What are the relevant cross-functional communities or networks?

Strategic Core

What's the goal of my strategy? What do I specifically want to achieve? What specifically do differently?

Activation

How can we listen systematically? What do we need to draw attention to? Where do we want to try out new things? How do we create sustainable activation? How do we measure success?

Narrative and the Big Picture

Figure 7: Illustration of the Strategy Activation Canvas 2023

What is the context of our strategy? What emotional and visual story do we want to tell? How can we appeal to all our senses? What is the visual language? What are the protagonists?

Fields of impact of the Canvas

The Strategy Activation Canvas unfolds along two fields of impact: The first field of impact relates to defining the context. It's about clarifying what is really at the core of a strategy. In a second step, visibility is created and those stakeholders are defined who can speed up a strategy or formulate a story. The second field of impact is acceleration. This means that activation mechanisms are established, which stand in the way with obstacles to strategy achievement or simply speed up certain topics and areas.

Fundamentally, strategy activation unfolds completely within these two fields of impact. When defining the context, it is important to clarify what the actual core of the strategy is in terms of content. While activation is ultimately targeted at entire teams or even companies, it is nonetheless vital for there to be a movement on the part of employees who go into motion and push and spread the activation. To make it possible, a narrative that is simple but carries strong content is required or a catchy image, which comes alive for good through different acceleration mechanisms.

These four areas (the strategic core, the movement, the narrative or Big Picture and the acceleration) constitute together the Strategy Activation Canvas. They form the very heart of any activation work. Alongside the two fields of impact, the Canvas also shows that prior strategy development and subsequent or parallel implementation are part of the Canvas, need to be part of it – although they're not part of the activation. Let's briefly explain the difference.

Demarcation of the Canvas

Strategy development

In our experience, the development of new strategic directions of impact still takes place in small groups. Sometimes it's done by including analyses and assessments from strategy and management consultants. Sometimes it's done with chosen internal stakeholders, e.g. the CEO and a small number of managers or one area manager and hand-picked colleagues from the executive team. This approach frequently results in papers with strong content, usually including market analyses and assessments, product/portfolio statements, specific financial assumptions and statements or even fields of action and specific project proposals. Such papers in such concentrated form provide us with an entry point to what we call the 'strategic core' in the Canvas – the first element of content-related strategy activation.

Strategy implementation

Strategy implementation on the other side of the Canvas refers to projects and initiatives that are necessary to achieve the objectives set out in the strategy. This may include projects, initiatives, an addition or disposal of teams or divisions, developing new products or adapting existing processes and operating models and far more. Basically everything that can be controlled and measured in a project portfolio. Companies that work with the Strategy Activation Canvas use information from the strategic core or mechanisms from the activation to manage the portfolio or give it a clear orientation.

Strategy Activation

This refers to the involvement of an entire workforce, independent of initiatives and change projects, in the strategy work and thus ultimately the exploitation of so-called social dynamics: Making use of all the things that usually block the way and creating a personal relationship to the strategy (see Chapter ➤ Social dynamics that prevent strategy implementation) – a relationship that is direct, doesn't require any previous knowledge and takes as a reference point a person's own role and his or her strengths and abilities. In summary, the aim is to make a strategy known and then make it a personal matter, for every single person in the company.

The special feature of the Strategy Activation Canvas is its universal character, its permeability to all types of methods and mechanisms (some of which we will showcase in this playbook). The Strategy Activation Canvas doesn't mean yet another theory, on the contrary: It complements well-known and proven models. This means it can easily be combined with all the good and well-functioning mechanisms already in use in companies. The Canvas only defines a framework that evolved from our work with major global organizations.

Let's go over the four fields on the next page. They will be discussed in greater detail in Chapter ➡ The fields of impact of the Strategy Activation Canvas: A guide for practitioners

Strategy development

Typical sequence

- Analyses (markets, customer wants & needs, competitors, processes, costs, etc.)

- Strategic options (attack, respond, split off, etc.)

- Decision-making process (typically with strategy experts, consultants, decision-makers, management board, administrative board, etc.)

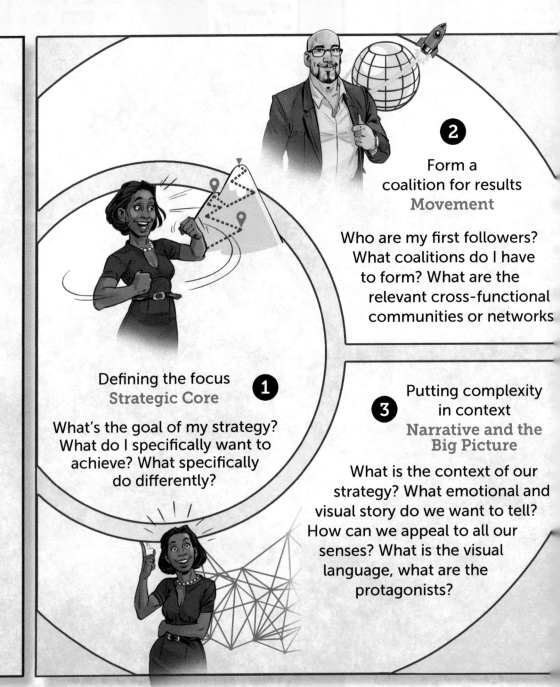

2 Form a coalition for results
Movement

Who are my first followers? What coalitions do I have to form? What are the relevant cross-functional communities or networks

Defining the focus
Strategic Core **1**

What's the goal of my strategy? What do I specifically want to achieve? What specifically do differently?

3 Putting complexity in context
Narrative and the Big Picture

What is the context of our strategy? What emotional and visual story do we want to tell? How can we appeal to all our senses? What is the visual language, what are the protagonists?

FIELD OF IMPACT
Defining the context

Figure 8:
Strategy Activation Canvas 2023

Involve the entire enterprise
Activation

4 How can we listen systematically?

5 What do we need
to draw attention to?

6 Where do we want to try out new things?

7 How do we create sustainable activation?

8 How do we measure success?

Implementation
of the strategy via
(selection)

- Initiatives,
  programs and
  projects

- Project
  portfolio
  management

- Objectives &
  Key Results
  (OKR)

- Impact,
  result and
  performance
  analyses

FIELD OF IMPACT
Accelerating strategy & transformation processes

If you want
people to care,
provide them
with context.

Robert Wreschniok

The Strategy Activation Canvas
Field of impact: Defining the context

Strategies are often intricate, concentrated documents. They typically require an explanation and must be embedded in a larger context. Even at board level, strategies are frequently the result of a structured dialog, of arguing and agreements, a discourse that is valuable but accessible to a small group only.

Defining the focus: The strategic core

Before a strategy can be put in a context that's accessible to broader swaths of an enterprise (see Chapter ➜ Putting complexity into context: The narrative and the Big Picture), it's vital to come to grips with its core first and answer the question: If I had to write the strategy on the nail of my thumb, what would it be about? Because with all the analytical background, shown options and the final decision to embark on a new path, the 'why' of the new strategy is often somewhat hidden in these documents. This doesn't mean that the core is not implicitly there, but in our experience,it's often eclipsed by all those 'milestones,' 'initiatives,' etc., which are explicitly formulated in the strategy paper.

The strategic core solely answers the question of 'why' – not what's obvious ('because our customers demand it,' 'because the markets are moving,' 'because it's making losses for us in our core business,' etc.) but, instead, the idea behind it, maybe even the deeper meaning there. It can be illustrated by a few examples:

- Amazon: '(...) To be the earth's most customer-centric company; to build a place where people can come to find and discover anything they might want to buy online.' There's nothing here about being a logistics firm or being a database provider.

- Apple: '(...) Developing technology at the interface of design and user-friendliness.' This also leaves open which technology, which markets, which customer groups.

- BMW: The car company is dedicated to the joy of driving. This strategy core then even justifies projects like improving the traffic flow in Munich – in order to achieve this joy. Obviously, not exactly an investment.

- Google: 'Making the information of this world accessible to all people at all times.' Although this leaves a lot of room to flesh it out, it has a very definite core.

- McDonald's: Every customer should leave the restaurant with a smile on his face. Thus the core does not focus on the food but on the experience.

- Starbucks: The core of the coffee chain is to create a so-called 'third place,' an expanded living room. In the United States, people refer to the first, the second and the third place, namely their home, their work place and – because their home often doesn't have this – a place where you can simply be. All initiatives and decisions the corporation takes are aligned to this core (cf. Howard Schultz 2011 in his book 'Onwards' – fascinating reading for how Starbucks was searching for a strategic core).

These examples show that the real core of a strategy is often rooted more deeply than any obvious development in terms of customer, market and earnings. The core is also linked to the history of a company, to pivotal leaders, visible and invisible employees, behaviors that are not documented anywhere and lots more. Bain & Company consultancy saw a direct link between searching for the core and sustainable and profitable growth, based on the same reasoning: If the core is unambiguous, clarity of the strategic leeway for options ensues nearly automatically (cf. Zook & Allen 2010 – with many fine examples of strategic cores).

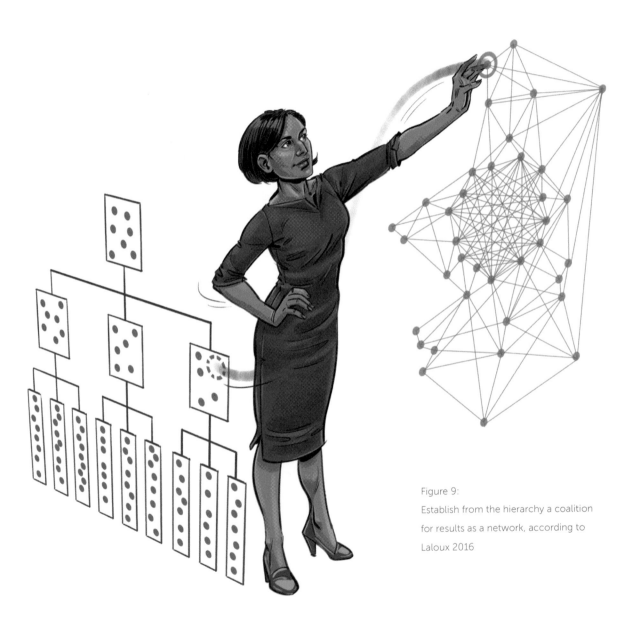

Figure 9:
Establish from the hierarchy a coalition
for results as a network, according to
Laloux 2016

Form a coalition for results: The movement

The second field of the Strategy Activation Canvas is all about expanding the contact points with the corporate strategy – ideally to the entire company. One crucial step consists of saying farewell to the notion that only a chosen group of insiders have access to the strategy. We consciously speak of three characteristics in this context: Coalition, results and movement.

If companies aren't agile, they are normally organized in segments – i.e. grouped around similar roles and skills or around markets, product segments, functional knowledge. This way of organizing comes from the 19th century (cf. Dignan 2019) and is based on the assumption that it makes a great deal of sense to consolidate and demarcate similar topics. It becomes manifest in the emergence of silos (without being judgmental – there are situations where they definitely make sense). Strategies, however, usually span across the different silos since they proclaim topics, trends, new paths – independent of a specific function or organizational unit.

This means you need the knowledge and experience of many different teams to make the impact of a new or renewed road visible. It's for this very reason that strategy activation jumps over the boundaries of existing segments and puts together all persons, roles, teams and communities that are relevant for achieving the strategy. That's what we mean with the metaphor of a coalition: Depending on the topic or initiative, a coalition is a composition of people and profiles, skills or experiences, needed for achieving a certain goal, which goes beyond reporting lines. As goals vary greatly, so do types of coalitions.

Such coalitions are defined by a common objective, a common vision, which needs to be formulated as specifically as possible. This is the second feature: Alignment with results. So it's not about establishing a group of people who initiate things more or less indiscriminately but about people who establish things throughout the company that have clear relevance to the new Big Picture. Typically, this can take the form of projects that are newly initiated or else are already working actively on existing parts of a strategy.

The third feature is that of a social movement. We have seen that coalitions sometimes gain momentum if they're left alone to act in peace (except for the shared vision, the common intent). 'Aligned autonomy' is this principle of agility, i.e. the role of executives is clearly one of getting out of the way (cf. Marquet 2013 'Greatness') and one often described in companies as 'empowerment': Independent action and letting go of control and monitoring.

This way, dynamics are created such as identifying, wanting to make a contribution – that last far longer than the membership to a particular coalition or team. This sophisticated formation of networks, coalitions, groups, teams, etc., is the task in the 'The Movement' field of the Strategy Activation Canvas.

Putting complexity into context: The narrative and the Big Picture
Strategy activation always tells a story, provides a picture or a metaphor. This step is crucial to making complexity tangible and accessible (without reducing or oversimplifying it) and giving it context. This is the third field of the Strategy Activation Canvas.

No strategy stands for itself. Every re-alignment, every investment in new business segments, every efficiency initiative and every turnaround have their own story. This story is important to understand because it explains the 'why' behind a change. At the same time, business leaders don't want to focus too much on the story, because it distracts from the target vision. ('What's made us successful so far won't necessarily be what will make us successful in the future' – except when you're dealing with a global roll-out of a product or service, which also needs to be adapted to local markets.) The story of an undertaking, i.e. looking back on what actually made us successful in the past and what were the topics where we failed (and that we absolutely must address), should become part of the strategy narrative. The same applies to the major influences from outside (e.g. market movements, macroeconomic conditions, trends in society, etc.) that make strategic development absolutely necessary. These three elements already show a strong rationale for the further development and appreciate the past; they showcase failure in terms of specific topics as valuable input for the way into the future.

Another part of the narrative is to highlight what makes people notice that they are not moving forward or stagnating; secondly, what makes people recognize that 100% of the goals have been achieved – from various perspectives (what makes customers realize it, investors, employees, etc.). These two elements identify important items, which may trigger a dialog on the path to strategy achievement. Measurement mechanisms can also be aligned to it to show quantitatively how well a strategy is doing.

The story of an undertaking should become part of the strategy narrative.

The one thing still missing here is a focus on today and thus on the most important priorities going forward. Organizations need a focus (which can change 100% over time) and need to know on which path the strategy is heading and what it means to the organization. For the latter, it's crucial not to explain in detail what it means to each function or business unit but to show quite consciously: What does this mean for the overall organization? This is the only way to convey the narrative of a movement and to prevent the story from consolidating silo structures.

Figure 10: Strategy told as narratives about the future of one's own organization and implemented as scenes on various Big Pictures, TATIN Institute 2023

The Strategy Activation Canvas
Field of impact: Accelerating strategy and transformation processes

The second field of impact of the Strategy Activation Canvas is designed to accelerate strategy and transformation processes. Thus it complements the first field of impact. We have deliberately separated it since mechanisms of impact change greatly when the context has been clarified. What we mean by this is: Defining the strategic core, setting up a coalition and working out the narrative revolve chiefly around content. The second field of impact relates to the topics of penetration, acceptance and enforcement in terms of the entire organization.

Hence the chapter on activation reads somewhat differently – here we mainly showcase mechanisms and concepts that can be combined as needed and are by no means conclusive. We'll present the selection we believe will help you – in the truest sense of the word – to activate teams or entire organizations. Combine them consciously with your own experience and the tools and formats deployed in your organization, try things out and develop them further. The only benchmark you ought to be guided by is: 'Do the means really serve the end of achieving our strategic goals more rapidly?' This is why you'll find few communicative tools such as newsletters, blogs, CEO emails, town-hall meetings, etc. – and even if they exist, it's only to show how to turn these tools into activation mechanisms. What then are the possibilities of activating teams and entire companies for a common strategy?

They consist in essence of a small number of mechanisms that can be applied to design activation and are based on a very fundamental logical chain of effects. (1) I need to listen; then (2) set a focus, before I (3) can sensualize and (4) experiment. What works well, I can (5) finalize, run permanently (partly in [6] digital form); and I can (7) measure its effectiveness.

Mechanisms of listening

Every activation commences with listening. The sources for this are manifold: So-called engagement surveys, often conducted several times a year, net promoter score, employee survey – we all are aware of numerous forms of information collection in companies. There is also the evaluation of the minutes of executive meetings; the observance of behavior; the interpretation of anecdotes and stories; even the evaluation of electronic calendars (based on anonymity, of course) or formats of communication/dialog between employees and managers. In short: From systematic surveys all the way to heuristic or rather free-floating formats – there are many ways of listening available to organizations today.

Alas, only a few make use of the facts thus established for activation work once the publication of the results has been digested. It can be fatal: The results are frequently a strong indication for those areas where things block the way of a strategy or where the strategy work can be significantly accelerated. We'll come back to the topic of measurability in a separate chapter of this Strategy Activation Canvas. At this point, we want to sum up and emphasize that surveys and evaluations of all types should be starting points for activation work.

Because if you begin the work of 'acceleration,' you'll see very soon: The human brain is basically a sort of 'defense machine': For evolutionary reasons, anything new is seen as risky. At a minimum, it's seen as questionable. So whenever you read or hear something new, the brain automatically compares it with what you already experienced, read or learned. And in areas where the new thing contradicts your experience, the brain says: 'Yes, but....'

Mechanisms of listening are about establishing ways of making use of this apparent negativity. Because when activating the strategy or transformation, social dynamics interact: 'I give you something new (strategy), you give me your experience ("Yes, but")'. This interaction can be systematized, and certain stakeholders can be used as 'ears.' Listening helps understand the 'defense machine' and is an important source for finding out what exactly needs to be activated: Why is a strategy not accepted? What exactly are the fears? Why is it permanently met with resistance? Etc.

If I want to accelerate, I must know where to accelerate. Accordingly, all acceleration begins with listening. Listening means employee surveys, ambassador programs, existing groups of 'change agents' or the analysis of the agenda of senior leadership groups (to learn what's currently on the mind of decision makers). All of these sources are a strong indicator of what actually must be 'activated' before you start accelerating.

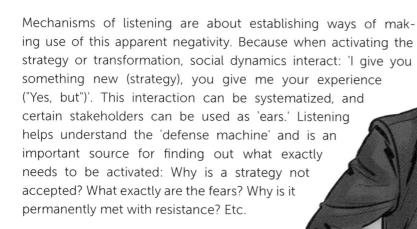

Focusing mechanisms

To carry forward strategies, transformation plans, major projects, etc., you don't need to have everything under control. On the contrary, a few but vital moments often suffice: If you change them thoroughly, existing behavior can be changed for good. This is really the idea behind the so-called 'moments that matter' (in some companies also referred to as 'moments of truth' or 'magic moments').

The idea is decades old and comes from marketing where people examine what situations are vital for building a brand and creating a particular brand experience. This means: Where and how should a customer perceive a brand so as to sense a specific brand experience in the long term. For transformation plans, the idea is similar. Ask yourself: 'What are the handful of meetings, phone calls, leadership situations, decision-making moments, etc., you have to change to make the entire project move in a different, new direction?' Then focus solely on those few moments.

Examples:

- Countless times we have seen that changing individual meetings results in permanently visible changes in the conduct of the staff of an entire business unit. For example, it is substantially more effective to transpose the agenda of a management team in order to trigger a particular discourse than to establish enormous voting governance.

- It is far more effective to retrain a small group of sales personnel in a particular moment of the sales process than to question or even turn the entire process inside out.

So ask yourself: What are the decisive moments for the strategic core (even if there are only one or two) that need to be (radically) changed. Then focus solely on the transformation of these moments.

Another mechanism of focus is the use of existing initiatives. Many companies (and external consultants) make the mistake of setting up and orchestrating a whole bunch of change mechanisms for every transformation project. This idea in particular was fleshed out, among others, in Kotter (cf. Kotter 2018), who argues: Every transformation agenda needs a change agenda.

And there is basically nothing wrong with this. Strategy activation, however, significantly expands the thinking here by involving existing initiatives and projects in the transformation agenda. Not as a parallel universe but completely integrated. Organizations are usually fully committed to 'business as usual,' and any change organization that is set up separately must face this corporate reality.

This is why the philosophy of strategy activation is to accelerate existing projects, models, processes, etc., and modify them such that they have crystal-clear relevance to the strategy. No change agenda is established. Instead, mechanisms are sought for how to alter existing realities cleverly so they make a contribution to the newly defined Big Picture. And all initiatives or parts of initiatives that have no relevance will be completely discontinued.

> What many successful strategy activations have in common is the tangible, specific and emotional character of the strategy.

Mechanisms of sensualization

What many successful strategy activations have in common is the tangible, specific and emotional character of the strategy. In nearly all companies we were able to examine, the format of a strategy is a Microsoft PowerPoint document. Sometimes they even have the same structure. Some companies present their strategies in the form of a prose text (probably so as to be more precise than a PowerPoint), but it doesn't happen very often.

The challenge of the format lies in the abstractness of the content: Strategies are reduced to (visualized) figures, some of which are complemented by conceptual frameworks. This means that understanding the content frequently requires prior knowledge in business management and finance, knowledge of the markets, experience and the ability to comprehend correlations in a structured way. Presenting the content in this format excludes a wider audience and reduces the potential for understanding.

To counteract this, one way is certainly not the right way: To reduce the well-thought-out content more and more to its bare bones. This usually doesn't do justice to the complexity of the content and ultimately will compromise the clarity of what the strategy is all about. So-called sensualization is a better approach, since it doesn't reduce the content but utilizes the mechanisms of storytelling and visualization to make it accessible to more people. Important: Without compromising content! Sensualization is the visualization of abstract concepts. Once a strategy can be penetrated with all senses, it becomes accessible to a broad audience; it can be discussed and even attacked. Above all, it can be experienced on an emotional level. The human brain captures 90% of knowledge through moving images, i.e. it can merge text, image, spoken words, mood, etc., in one fell swoop (cf. Thesmann 2016). This is precisely why strategies should be made conceivable with all the senses: To be understood cognitively and emotionally.

Only then can we see how they relate to ourselves and deal with the question: 'What exactly is my role in making the strategy possible?' To answer that question I must initially comprehend the quality of content that goes far beyond bullet points and infographics. Successful strategy activation thus means presenting a focused essence of the strategy in a sensualized way. Sensualization commences where communication ends. First of all, the target audience of a strategy must understand it.

That's difficult to achieve if all you have is intricate and detailed expert papers, which are usually narrated in town-hall meetings in a top-down manner. At the same time, knowledge of a strategy is necessary for creating one's own or the team's contribution to the strategy.

Knowing the strategy is only the beginning. What about not only understanding strategies but also internalizing them? Making it the benchmark of daily action – without thinking too much about it? It's possible if content is sensualized and above all symbolized. Strategy activation turns the core of the strategy to a message in the form of a story, an image, a metaphor, which then becomes the reference point for interactions, priorities, dialog, etc., throughout the company (see Chapter ➲ Putting complexity in context: The narrative and the Big Picture). This symbolization is the central complement to the narration of PowerPoint slides, which is the predominant mechanism for making strategy visible in so many organizations.

Mechanisms of experimentation

The idea struck us for the first time with Google: To conduct small, controlled experiments, learn from them and reflect on them. 'What does this mean for the Big Picture?' is much more efficient than designing a solution on the drawing board just to find out in the end: 'That's actually not what we want or need.' Seems obvious, but the reality in companies is often different: Change processes are still frequently designed on the drawing board and than rolled out all over the place.

Two things are decisive for setting up controlled experiments: First, reflect upon matters in a structured way and make the findings available to the other teams; second, abort an experiment if it doesn't deliver the expected results. Many teams make the mistake of putting more and more on the agenda without a step of honest reflection and/or the courage to end things. Amazon, for instance, had the courage to discard the project of its 'Fire Phone' mobile when it didn't prove to be a market success. But then they reflected on the matter, and the same development team designed 'Amazon Echo,' which was a resounding success – an impressive example of the courage to stop, learn and take a different path on the basis of what's been learned (cf. Velasco 2018 and Clifford 2020).

On the other hand, experimental mechanisms run the risk of establishing a system of experiments that rarely turn out to end in a global roll-out. When experiments are successful and offer the possibility to make a contribution across the board, then this step is decisive: To abandon the realm of experiment and launch the results globally.

Agile mechanisms

The times when change processes in companies were planned and implemented with military precision haven't vanished and certainly are justified with some topics. But they're becoming more and more irrelevant when it comes to achieving complex and global overall strategies that have several and ever changing variables. Hence an agile mode is at the heart of strategy activation. In the following, we want to present a few important mechanisms that help to tackle topics and achieve results in a short period of time:

- ✅ Cross-functional teams, i.e. picking people and roles such that they solve a problem (not the other way round: Bringing tasks to existing teams).

- ✅ The 'customer' is part of the team, i.e. those for whom a solution is being developed must be integrated in the development teams.

- ✅ Intervals, i.e. recurring time windows (or time boxes); for instance, to meet every x weeks (usually two) and show what has been achieved ('sprint,' 'retrospective') and to meet every y weeks (usually twelve) to plan the next larger time period together ('release').

- ✅ Employees provide as much time as they can, i.e. not all employees have to provide 100% of their time. Instead, it should be determined how much everybody can provide and, on the basis of this amount ('capacity'), only to take on what they can achieve ('load').

- ✅ Prioritize based on value, i.e. reflecting on the question regularly (see Chapter ➡ The 11 agile principles of strategy activation) of what will bring value at this moment or in this sprint and de-prioritizing all else. This dialog must be repeated over and over again.

Digital mechanisms

It has certainly been an everyday feature at many global corporations for some time now; for some companies, it probably only became visible during the COVID-19 pandemic: Working together 'face to face' in one room is not always possible or even wise. Workshop formats, collaborative formats, the presentation of information, learning together or individually – all of this can be done with (sometimes free) digital tools today. This even applies to production employees. Here it's important to provide the infrastructure.

Digital collaboration is subject to different dynamics than working on topics together in one room. In his contribution to the five levels of virtual collaboration, Glaveski (cf. Glaveski 2000) describes how 'copying' the office situation into a virtual set-up meets at best the second of a total of five possible maturity levels – because all inefficiencies are also copied without making use of the digital world to get rid of them. Instead of merely copying, people should adapt to the digital formats of collaboration (e.g. working together in documents, working with collaboration tools). Teams that succeed in working completely asynchronously go one step further. They establish a culture defined by common goals, work principles and results – beyond that, the team members work completely independently (cf. Choudhury 2020 'Our Work-from-Anywhere Future'). According to Glaveski, the nirvana is teams that actually collaborate better without an office. The studies of Choudhury also show that such setups are quite possible.

Why are we describing these levels? Because we want to demonstrate that digital setups have advantages for collaboration if they're used correctly and don't just imitate the office setup. This is true not only for global corporations that are accustomed to this kind of collaboration but also for companies that see themselves suddenly forced to find new ways of collaboration due to a pandemic such as COVID-19; or for companies that want to reduce their CO_2 footprint strategically, so collaboration in one room no longer is an option. Digital mechanisms are technically so mature today that there's no need for compromises in terms of results or activation.

Measurement mechanisms

The language of top management is and will remain the language of facts, and that's a good thing. Because this is the only way to show how successful a strategy has been. This also applies to strategy activation. Measurement mechanisms in the most basic sense make strategy work visible, e.g. by carrying out a 'zero measurement' (i.e. how many employees have understood a strategy and think they're able to make a personal contribution). Or the measurement of commitment, an indicator that is frequently measured, especially in major corporations.

> The best-known example of this is the network analysis that shows the power of the networks of individual employees.

In a wider sense, elements of strategy activation can also be refined by means of mature measurement methods. The most prominent example of this is the network analysis that shows the strength of the networks of individual employees (through the analysis of meetings and emails) – highlighting who in the company is really a key person for inducing enthusiasm for an idea among employees and engaging them.

At the same time, measurements reach their limits. In discussions with the managing directors of large corporations, they frequently express things like teams 'seem' to collaborate better or that a 'spirit of optimism' prevails. Such statements cannot really be expressed in figures but count nonetheless. Working with qualitative statements, discussions in focus groups or a pulse check with all employees during a town-hall meeting are therefore important indicators for the success or failure of a strategy activation.

The Strategy Activation Canvas
The activation lie: When activation is not an activation

By now, strategy activation has become an established feature in many places, with clearly different characteristics: From quite impressive activation architectures that cover entire global workforces (see Chapter ➜ Microsoft: Help shaping a new era – activating Microsoft's strategic core worldwide) all the way to a so-called 'camouflage activation,' i.e. the label says 'activation' but it's nothing but old wine in new skins. It's therefore worthwhile to take a peek behind the terminology of a strategy activation:

- ✓ Do the formats allow for the shared development of contents, or are given contents implemented/rolled out?

- ✓ Do the formats allow for documented dialogs that are open-ended and from which people learn from one another, or do the results of dialog formats just disappear in some PowerPoint documentation?

- ✓ Do the formats provide employees with the necessary tools and mechanisms to work on solutions on their own, or are they ready-made solution mechanisms or stories/parts of stories that will be rolled out globally?

A dialog not progressively continued is the best indicator of camouflage activation, i.e. the strategy is talked about and ideas are bandied forth but in the end, following the dialog, it's exactly like it was before the dialog in terms of strategy momentum. Even the development of images of dialog or visual strategy stories do not yet constitute an activation: If the images trigger narration and not joint development, again before the dialog is merely after the dialog: Although there is insight (the direction toward which one's own actions are to go), an entire generation of managers and employees is absent.

Strategy is the exciting story about the future of one's own company.

Robert Wreschniok

Figure 12: Rethinking leadership while jointly building the future, illustrated in a Big Picture, TATIN Institute 2023

THE FIELDS OF IMPACT
OF THE STRATEGY
ACTIVATION CANVAS

The fields of impact of the Strategy Activation Canvas
A guide for practice

The areas of the Strategy Activation Canvas provide the conceptual framework of strategy activation, i.e. they help bring strategy activation initiatives into a sequence and a system. In particular, when major strategic projects are ahead. At the same time, the sequence is not dogmatic; the fields do not have to be followed in order to activate a strategy. Each individual building block stands for itself and by itself creates significant value already. While the first three areas set the context, the fourth outlines acceleration and maintaining the dynamics.

The Strategy Activation Canvas deliberately does not start with strategy formulation but, instead, sets in once a strategy has been formulated and is on hand. To activate (large) organizations, it is a good idea first,

1. **to have clarity in terms of the strategic core,** i.e. to elaborate what the strategy is actually about. Two vital building blocks are derived from it:

2. Clarify how the entire **organization can be involved as a social movement** with

3. a **powerful narrative**.

4. With these building blocks, the **architecture of the acceleration** can be built, controlled and embedded on a long-term basis.

While (1), (2) and (3) define the area of impact of setting a context, thus activation work that determines content, (4) refers to the actual acceleration of the strategy.

But the Canvas works well also without following this sequence: For example, once the core is clear and the 'only' thing missing is a common language for the strategy that is global and uniform, then a (3) powerful narrative suffices to create focus. Or projects and initiatives are already being managed as a portfolio to achieve the strategy; in this case, understanding the (2) social movement may be enough to increase its speed. Depending on the projected strategy, the building blocks form a sequence or stand alone.

All building blocks that we present in the four fields exist already; the Strategy Activation Canvas deliberately does not propose to be a new theory. On the contrary: It covers a wide range of powerful and tried-and-tested mechanisms, methods and schemes, some of which have been applied to strategy and organizational development for decades. The playbook compiles a selection of the most vigorous concepts and arranges them such that they unfold in a powerful overall work. There certainly are other schemes that can be seamlessly integrated with the four building blocks described above.

The fields of impact of the Strategy Activation Canvas
Defining the focus: The strategic core

One vital aspect of strategy activation is to ensure that people actively work toward a goal in a coordinated way. The development of a strategic core as a story is a decisive acceleration factor for achieving this goal and hence is the first element of the Strategy Activation Canvas.

Strategic Core

What's the goal of my strategy? What do I specifically want to achieve? What specifically do differently?

Figure 13: Illustration of the Strategy Activation Canvas 2023

Case study: Hamburg Commercial Bank | Transformation #PushForResults

Kaja Wilkniss

In 2018, Hamburg Commercial Bank (HCOB) embarked on a journey that no bank ever had undertaken in Germany prior to that. The former HSH Nordbank became Hamburg Commercial Bank. For the first time in the German banking landscape, a regional state bank was sold to private owners and a completely new path was taken that required a comprehensive transformation of the entire organization. HCOB has undergone a profound transformation over the last three years and is today successfully operating on the market as a focused special financier and profitable commercial bank.

The honed business strategy also entailed a realignment of the brand and an in-depth change in the corporate culture at all organizational levels: From a bank owned by the federal states of Hamburg and Schleswig-Holstein, which went through difficult times due to the financial market and shipping crisis, had had to grapple with inherited liabilities and was predominantly hierarchically organized, toward a culture of actively shaping things, with notably more responsibility for each individual, i.e. ownership of tasks, issues and projects. Flatter hierarchies and clearly-defined efficiency targets were by no means a matter of course for many employees and were to be embedded in the new bank. Many ways were entirely new to the bank or were actually created from scratch while doing things. Why shall we do it, what shall we do, and how shall we do it?

The goal of the two-year activation scheme, which was aligned with the target of 'action expresses priorities' and was organized in agile sprints, was the creation of a uniform understanding of the strategic goals (WHY), the individual results (WHAT) as well as the implementation in day-to-day work (HOW). The arrangement was supposed to be translated directly to goal-oriented and results-oriented actions, even if all agenda items were not clearly defined yet. For me, as the manager of the 'Change' workstream, one of the greatest challenges was: Focusing on what employees already knew and can do and not on what will be resolved and become (more) clear only later. The agile approach in sprints allowed the management and us as the project team from Corporate Strategy and Human Resources to adapt the ongoing transformation process again and again based on prioritization and to define expectations and goals for each sprint in a new and clear way. To achieve a change in the culture, in the context of the introduction of meritocratic principles, a common currency of success was defined right at the onset: Results.

To convey, in a first step, the strategic objectives and the WHY, HOW and WHAT and embed them firmly in day-to-day work, a disruptive approach was adopted. And to leave behind old patterns of presentations, we used the 'Big Picture' here. Based on this illustration, we told the exciting story of the bank: Starting with the solid foundation laid in the past, to the challenges and transformation of the present day, all the way to the vision of the future for the new bank. Sensitive issues such as the financial crisis, uncertainty on account of the new, private owners, the intended reduction of the workforce and the daily 'mindset challenge' for management and employees were mapped transparently in the story. The goal was to work through these topics. The entire organization was encouraged to tackle the challenges. Looking at the 'Big Picture,' every employee should be able to trace the path of the bank and tell a similar similar story, i.e. his or her story.

#pushforresults – results count

To involve the employees closely in the development of the 'Big Picture,' scenes of the future were painted in co-creative workshops. Following the target of 'How do our customers, our executives and our employees recognize success?', the future part of the map was created that served as a guide from then on. A strategic core message of the 'Big Picture' was that the bank can only handle the path forward that stands for a successful future on the map if it delivers the required results. A bank-wide supportive campaign was derived with the hashtag #pushforresults.

To tie in closely with the day-to-day work of employees, a cross-functional team from nearly all departments of Hamburg Commercial Bank was formed, the so-called 'Result Agents.' They were and still are ambassadors and multipliers of the transformation and they have brought results and insights from discussions, e.g. with the board or the HR project team, to the entire organization. At the same time, they acted as a sounding board, capturing the mood and questions from employees and giving us on the project as well as the whole management team a representative picture of the progress and how the new corporate culture is being accepted. The 'Results Agents' are still acting as mediators today between management and employees. They fulfill their job as a sounding board and are active in both directions.

To boost the exchange of ideas with leaders, who are important motivators for achieving the transformation goals, a number of cross-divisional and cross-departmental events for managers took place, called 'Push for Results' meetings. The status of the transformation as well as line and company subjects were reported and discussed. Then there were bank-wide town-hall meetings to provide all employees with an overview of the transformation milestones already achieved and an outlook on the challenges of the next few months.

97

To assess the efficacy of the activation measures systematically, a survey among the employees was initiated. For the development needs identified in the various divisions, measures were drawn up that could help to strengthen employees' identification with the strategy.

I had a great time developing the 'Big Picture' together on the team and was positively surprised at how well it was accepted and adopted by the board, the leaders and my colleagues. The 'big colorful picture' is appealing, sparks discussions and has been used in many forms in our bank. It was and is a new and vivid way for us to gather everybody in the company behind a target image – in the truest sense of the word.

Figure 14: Big Picture of the Hamburg Commercial Bank about the successful transformation of a regional state bank to a private-sector bank.

Define the core: Strategy as a narrative

Only 18% of the middle managers responsible for implementing the strategy are able to explain the company's key strategic goals coherently. 95% of employees don't even know the strategy of their own company (cf. Sull, Sull & Yoder 2018 and Ernst & Young 2019)[4]. What's fatal here: Most people find it difficult to become enthusiastic about things they don't understand. Conversely, the commitment of employees can be visibly boosted if you create a clear understanding of what they're supposed to commit to (cf. empirically).

The case study of Allianz in this playbook (see Chapter ➡ Case study: Allianz #lead – What makes a great leader?) is an excellent example of this. It can be proven and statistically sustained how the group increased by almost 100% the so-called performance enablement index and 54% the commitment index within two years through the inspiring communication of a) where the company's new journey is heading and b) what personal contribution each employee can make to the transformation. This example shows impressively that, to supplement the actual strategy paper, its narrative and the broad involvement of the workforce have a crucial impact on how successful a strategy will ultimately be.

What then is a strategy in the form of a narrative? Let's assume that every strategy starts with an idea of the future. It contains elements of a narrative about the creation of new opportunities and the design of a new corporate reality. We further assume that all strategies in principle have the possibility to succeed.

And they constitute the cornerstones of strategic narratives: Successful strategies that inspire people and give them hope are often stories about the future of their company in a world worth living in. These strategies thus follow a 'law' of successful narration that was characterized by a famous American author as follows: If a story is not about the audience, it won't listen. And thus I define a rule: A great and engrossing story is about everybody and about yourself – or it won't last.

It is undoubtedly challenging to develop a narrative that resolves around every listener, every reader and around yourself as well. It's likely to become even more difficult if this story isn't fictional but real. If it's not about filling empty pages but about real life: The real future of my own company, the shaping of markets and products and, above all, of the people who are to make all this a reality. It's clear from this that the value of a successful strategy is not to be measured by the quantitative goals alone but also by the number of its followers: The more people you as a leader can involve in the success of a strategy, i.e. the more people work for a common goal in a coordinated way, the more valuable it will be.

If a story is not about the audience, it won't listen. And thus I state a rule: A great and engrossing story is about everyone and about yourself – or it won't last.

One of the most apt requirements for a good story was formulated by Jonah Sachs (cf. Sachs 2012): A good story is:

Tangible – A good story presents information in such a way that it can be comprehended quickly. People can 'feel' or 'see' it. So does your story post answers to: Who?, what?, where? and when?

Relevant – Good stories are important to us when we want to see characters or values in the story either rewarded or else punished. Can one identify with your story because one understands the motives?

Powerful – Good stories give the impression that you share an experience. Can people learn something from your story for their own life or for their own work area?

Memorable – Stories use rich scenes and metaphors that can be remembered without much thought. Does your story leave a lasting impression?

Emotional – Stories boost emotional commitment (yes, even stories for a dry strategy that is based on financial key figures). Does your story lead to people feeling something and not just knowing something?

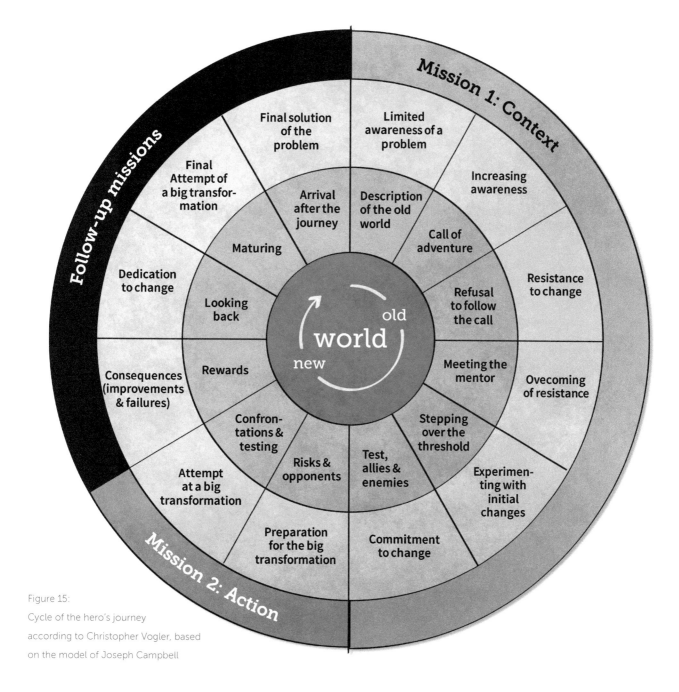

Figure 15:

Cycle of the hero's journey

according to Christopher Vogler, based

on the model of Joseph Campbell

The labels within the figure, from outer to inner rings:

Mission 1: Context

Mission 2: Action

Follow-up missions

- Limited awareness of a problem
- Increasing awareness
- Resistance to change
- Ovecoming of resistance
- Experimenting with initial changes
- Commitment to change
- Preparation for the big transformation
- Attempt at a big transformation
- Consequences (improvements & failures)
- Dedication to change
- Final Attempt of a big transformation
- Final solution of the problem

Middle ring:
- Description of the old world
- Call of adventure
- Refusal to follow the call
- Meeting the mentor
- Stepping over the threshold
- Test, allies & enemies
- Risks & opponents
- Confrontations & testing
- Rewards
- Looking back
- Maturing
- Arrival after the journey

Center:
old
world
new

But how exactly do you design a good story so that it's tangible, memorable, emotional, etc.? Let's take a closer look.

Capture the core: The most important actors as a source
First of all, what's most important: To shape a strategic narrative, you don't need to be all that skillful at creative writing. What you have to do is pose a few key questions and then listen carefully. Let's now walk through all the steps necessary for a good story.

The first question is about the actors: Who are the most important people I need for the successful implementation of my strategic goals (...a great and interesting story is about everyone and yourself or it will not last...)? Most people answer this question hierarchically: 'I myself and my "direct reports" and maybe a couple of aspiring and up-and-coming talents.'

But is that really the case? Are these really the most important people for successful strategy implementation?

Who actually are the most important people I need to achieve my strategic goals?

In our view, the question about the most important actors can't be answered via the hierarchy alone or across-the-board via other clearly-defined categories. However, it has a lot to do with the core of your strategic considerations. Let's look at it from different angles:

- Who is ultimately to be reached with the strategy?

- Just the top leaders or a lot more people?

- Who exactly must 'deliver' the strategy?

- Whom will it affect most, whom least?

- Who will oppose it or even torpedo it?

Regardless of supporters or opponents who can't be avoided, the question remains: 'Who exactly are the key players needed for the successful implementation of your strategy?' It looks simple at first glance. What we experienced: The question of who is actually needed for the success of a strategy is rarely asked in the first place; or the answer to it is not worked with actively.

We have seen that, depending on the size of the organization, around 20 to 40 persons play the role of just exactly these key people (not all of them need to be employees: Think of customers, business partners or investors). Making a list of these people is the first step for getting closer to the core of your strategy.

Get to know your own strategy better through systematic questions – to be able to tell an exciting story of the future.

Understand the core: A look behind the strategy paper
In the next step, you'll take this group of people and get to the bottom of your strategy and draw an picture that lies behind the written word.

One way is to approach the core with in-depth interviews. In the following, we present the question clusters that help you understand the core of a strategy. We have had positive experience with conducting 'neutral' interviews, i.e. talking to people outside the business area (or company) concerned. And with conducting 'confidential' conversations. After all, it's ultimately not important from whom the answers come. As described in Chapter ➜ Putting complexity in context: The narrative and the Big Picture, the story will later be told independently of existing organizational units or teams (they have been purposely omitted in the picture because you want to tell story from the point of view of the entire company).

Such in-depth interviews typically last about one to one and a half hours. There is no 'right' or 'wrong' in the answers. Because the questions aren't about factual knowledge but about embeddedness, assessment, a personal view. Every interviewee is to speak whatever comes in mind first, because that means it's in the forefront of his or her current perception. The validation is performed later by an anonymized semantic comparison of the content in the answers of all interviewees. This means: The more frequently key statements are made, the more they seem to shape the way the interviewees think and act.

The following question clusters are not random. Their sequence follows the basic principles of narration: If you conducted the conversation well and have the questions and answers read to you aloud by one of the interlocutors, you will see that you already have a perspective of the strategy as an exciting story about the future.

What are the major trends?

`The first cluster of questions` should clarify the context of your strategy. This is about the major trends, global topics that are easily accessible to everybody – after all the company moves within these trends in the world, in society and on the market. Above all, you're looking for trends that your employees feel themselves and that evidently have something to do with the future of your organization.

On the track of pluralism

Important for the conversation: When a trend is mentioned, ask directly for an example to illustrate the trend. Because that's the actual information you want to understand. For example: An interviewee mentions the trend of 'digitization.' This catchphrase is far too broad and abstract to be filled with content later – everyone in the company has an idea about it, but the views on the matter can differ widely. The example you ask for allows you to describe a scene that you can intuitively understand. For example: 'In the future, our products will be bought solely online, and there won't be stores anymore.'

The problem in many strategy papers is the 'consensus subjects.' Here the challenge is: How do you bring them to life in organizations?

This is where it gets exciting: The next interlocutor who also sees 'digitization' as one of the three most important trends might give you the following example: 'With smart algorithms that measure the behavior of our customers, we'll be able to develop a completely new range of offers.'

One trend. Two completely different answers and thus manifestations. The point is: Both are neither wrong nor right. They're personal beliefs. But it's these beliefs that will impact their actions when implementing the strategy. If the differences in viewpoints aren't talked about, there will be conflict. Later, when it becomes apparent that the strategy doesn't work, people will talk of an 'island solution' or will say: 'We act in an uncoordinated way' or 'There's a hidden agenda.' The aim of the trend question (and all the following questions) is to understand the different meanings behind trend catchphrases.

Take different points of view
How do I recognize a catchphrase? There's a simple rule of thumb: Any word that cannot be drawn is too abstract and thus tends to be a catchphrase: 'Love,' 'strategy,' 'digitization,' 'customer focus,' 'innovation.' All these words cannot be drawn. Try it out in the next email you send to a colleague. Underline all the words that cannot be drawn because they're abstract words. You'll be surprised.

Words like 'strategy' or 'innovation,' etc., are not incredibly complicated. Everybody understands them. Everybody has a clear meaning they give to the catchphrase. Everybody uses the words, hardly anybody questions them. And that's where the problem lies: Frequently, the meanings people associate with a word are completely different, which then leads to misunderstandings or even diverging decisions.

Because every abstract word opens up leeway for interpretation. And not all people see this leeway as something positive. The goal of strategy activation at a later stage is to form coalitions and spark enthusiasm in them to work jointly for the corporate future. If this future is interpreted in many different ways right from the onset, it's robbed of firepower straightaway – because ultimately people will not act in concert but everybody will do their own thing. It is particularly fatal if this discord pre-dominates on the leadership team, because then the disagreement is cemented by the leadership role. Sometimes not even consciously.

Take the example of 'strategy': Sure, chess pieces being moved has become an established image for strategy. But do chess pieces say anything about your specific strategy, the unique goal you personally pursue? Only when we ask people to explain their strategy specifically can we get from the abstract to the graspable.

Recognize and use pictorial language
The final note on the question about trends is about how to recognize metaphors and the pictorial language used. The results from this exploratory phase finally flow into a story or a picture (see Chapter ➜ Putting complexity in context: The narrative and the Big Picture). The content is already there within your organization: Do your interlocutors speak of 'Put some horsepower on the road'? Do they say 'Then we can really take off'? Or 'We must get out of the machine room?' All these are metaphors that are extremely valuable for later activation work, so listen carefully.

What experience have you had here?

The second cluster of questions should explore the history, so you ask questions about the past. Questions that help you to detect collective experiences, good and bad: What impressive things have we achieved in our history? Where did we really hit the wall?

Asking this question has two advantages. First, you learn about key strengths, on which you can build later, and weaknesses that should be made visible to avoid them in the future. Secondly, the question entails a certain appreciation of your interlocutor's personal biography: Your experience is critical to make the corporate strategy successful.

Shaping the future with knowledge of the past.
This question aims at linking past challenges and solutions with the challenges the organization is facing. So: What have you learned from your mistakes or achievements, which are crucial for drawing up our picture of the future? Accordingly, the answers you receive can be formulated in two different scenarios of the story later. (1) If we made it then, we'll make it again all the more in terms of what lies ahead. Or: (2) Since we had to learn painfully in the past that it doesn't work this way, we'll try another path in the future.

Examples related to (1) conveying pride, focusing on one's own strengths and reinforcing identity. However, more important for the later activation of the strategy are all examples of projects or initiatives that did not lead to the desired success in the past. Because what's shown here (2) are: sovereignty (we're open to our mistakes), willingness to learn (we can do better) and justification of new ways (so we'll try the following).

An example in the context of 'innovation' is the realization during an activation project run by a major internationally active publishing house that all magazines brought to market in the last 80 years had one thing in common: They all existed already as functioning niche products on the market.

They were discovered by the publisher, bought, developed and became leading magazines in their respective fields. Those who are aware of this innovation DNA don't lock in their best editors in a meeting room for weeks on end so they come up with a new title but search for auspicious magazines to make them great in accordance with a tried-and-tested pattern. This is a completely different way of implementing a growth strategy because you have listened carefully to past experience.

How to get to the heart of the matter?
The third cluster of questions relates to essence: How would you explain to a new colleague who asks you the key goals of the strategy summed up in three sentences? These and similar questions help clarify whether the most important people you need to execute your strategy actually have the same strategic goals in mind as you do. The degree of understanding and consensus is queried in this section. The 'random encounter' with the young colleague in the hallway is important, so no long lectures take place and every interlocutor can get to the heart of the new strategy. In the subsequent strategy activation, when the story is framed, it's crucial to make it simple. The answers to this question constitute a pool of ideas on how to get to this simplicity in terms of language and imagery.

If everything stays that way?

The fourth cluster of questions helps to derive a so-called 'case of urgency'. By describing what will happen if everything stays the same, the arguments for the urgency of the strategy are honed even further. In addition, the question creates awareness of the content of the story that is later to be told: Namely that the strategy also has the purpose of averting staying in the here and now. At the same time, the answers show where resistance to the new strategy may crop up (especially if the interlocutors don't see any major risks in the event that the strategy fails or don't see the strategy as so relevant that it would really result in changes).

What does success actually mean?

The fifth cluster of questions looks at the end. For this, thought experiments are a good thing: 'Imagine that the new strategy will be 100% successful in five years' time. How would employees, leaders and customers recognize it?' The question is both the easiest and the most difficult of the eight questions. Easy because most interviewees immediately come up with a plethora of answers. Difficult when they are asked to substantiate the answers with specific examples. Then things are no longer so obvious.

Typical answers you will hear: 'Well, that's as clear as day. We will have seen significant growth. With respect to digitization and especially customer orientation, we'll clearly have a headstart on our competitors and we'll be able to drive innovations much faster to the market than today.'

A recent supplement to the triad of digitization, customer orientation and innovation is the wish to help improve the quality of life of people/customers. So much for the easy part of the answer. The challenging part that usually leads to a longer phase of thinking and contemplating is the follow-up question: How will customers know that we are much more customer-oriented than anybody else? What do they experience with us that they don't experience with other companies?

Like the example of digitization, answers will vary greatly: 'Customers will have a completely different premium experience at the point of sale. You have to imagine it like you have seen with Apple products in a store for electrical and electronic devices. The Apple products stand out totally.' And: 'With us, customers will be involved as early as with the conceptual ideas for new offers. We'll design things not for customer needs but all along the line of customer needs.'

Again, two very smart answers as examples of a new form of customer orientation. Both are neither right nor wrong. Both are beliefs on how customer orientation can be recognized in case the strategy is 100% successful. The decisive factor for activation here is again to make the meaning visible that lies behind the abstract terms.

Now boss – and then?

The sixth cluster of questions involves consciously changing roles: The interviewee is appointed as the new CEO. What would he or she do in an executive position? With such and similar questions, you clarify the different priorities in the minds of your interlocutors: What would have to happen first – here and now? A range of possible priorities can be derived from the answers. It goes without saying that the answers aren't the cause of an initiative. However, the answers can be compared with existing plans, can augment them or identify white spots in the planning.

> How will customers know that we are much more customer-oriented than anybody else?

After all, the answers reflect the opinions of the most important people you need for the implementation of your strategy (see Chapter ➔ Capture the core: The most important actors as a source).

What if we just can't get it done?
The seventh cluster of questions focuses on failure. Many people have a hard time describing precisely how employees or customers would identify success; describing how the implementation of the strategy will fail is far easier. It's fascinating that the strategy itself is rarely questioned; socio-dynamic effects dominate the range of responses (see Chapter ➔ Social dynamics destroy strategy activation): Not enough coordination on the leadership team; departmental or silo thinking; people don't feel they're involved; decisions aren't consistently translated into action and lots more. None of these are reasons for a new strategy but vital aspects that absolutely need to be taken into account for the activation. Because again it's true: If 26 out of 30 interlocutors state 'lack of coordination on the leadership team' as a possible reason for failure, then this obstacle must become a part of the activation strategy. We talk about 'gold nuggets' here that are dug out. The question about failure yields extremely valuable clues about stumbling blocks during activation. Detecting them early on helps with adapting the activation mechanisms.

How do you recognize the new mindset?
<mark>The eighth cluster of questions</mark> ties in directly with the seventh question about failure: What attitudes and what mindset can prevent these problems from cropping up? The question aims at getting to the bottom of the problems that are feared.

You can pose your question by asking interviewees: 'Please formulate sentences that contain "from" ... "to"' to hone down statements. For example: 'From looking for a guilty party to looking for solutions together.' This addresses the lack of a culture of dealing with errors. A knee-jerk reaction when something went wrong is first to find and punish the wrongdoer and not to look forward and expend thought on what can be learned from the mishap or even how to benefit from it. Or: 'From processing tasks to jointly developing ideas'. This statement refers to a lack of a culture of service and innovation – we receive instructions from the business units and process them as quickly as possible. Or ...

Summarize the core: The discourse with management
The time has come: You've conducted about 30 interviews and thus have collected 30 exciting stories about the future of your own company. Stories about the major trends driving society and our markets (question 1); how we dealt with such challenges in the past more or less successfully, and what lessons we learned from it (question 2). What would happen if we simply continued as before (question 3); and how we get to the point of the most important goals to prevent it (question 4). Then we described how we would identify success in concrete terms and how customers, employees and managers actually identify success (question 5); and what is the fastest path to success (question 6). It won't be an easy journey (question 7); but together and with the right mindset (question 8), we can do it.

To consolidate the individual statements into an Big Picture, you put the answers next to one another and conduct a semantic analysis. The anonymized answers to each question are compared and clustered into contexts according to meaning. This reduces the number of individual answers, and initial group preferences or very different interpretations can be recognized from one and the same cluster of questions. The result of the analysis is then discussed with the initiators of the strategy (e.g. the management board or supervisory board).

One thing is achieved in any case: All thoughts, perspectives and opinions about the strategy are now on the table. And what's best of all: They can now be discussed, weighed and prioritized neutrally without the rank or function of the author being known. Now the discussion no longer is conducted along consensus terms such as 'digitization,' 'customer orientation,' 'innovation' or 'quality of life' (who would be against these fine words?) but, instead, at one level below: How would success in these dimensions be recognized in tangible terms? What are the most important steps in this direction? What experiences can we build upon, and so on.

From this alignment process, an exciting narrative about the company's future is slowly developed. A strategy about a possible future of the company, the shaping of markets and range of offers and, above all, about the people who will experience all this and are motivated to make it a reality.

The result from this discourse as a whole becomes a part of the story and the visual Big Picture (see Chapter ➲ Putting complexity in context: The narrative and the Big Picture). Next we would like to take a look at the networks in which strategy activation gains momentum.

How do you know that you're on the right track?
`The strategic core`

When you begin talking about the purpose of the strategy during strategy activation, then...

- the key actors have shared their understanding in terms of the benefits, the tangible added value and the associated achievements of the strategy.

- you will have minimized interpretation leeway, construals and misunderstandings based on abstract terms and representations.

- you will have achieved cohesion through the involvement of key people, thus creating ideal conditions for later activation.

- you will be aware of the knowledge, attitudes and expectations of the key people and have condensed them into a shared Big Picture.

You never lose.
You either win or learn.

Nelson Mandela

The fields of impact of the Strategy Activation Canvas Form a coalition for results: The movement

S o far, the core of the strategy has become clear in all its facets: From financial metrics all the way to the stumbling blocks hidden in the corporate culture. While the previous chapter describes how to formulate a coordinated narrative that directly includes people, this chapter will deal with the question of how to build a so-called movement, i.e. with the question of how the narrative can be enshrined throughout the company. This anchor is the second element of the Strategy Activation Canvas in the 'Context' field.

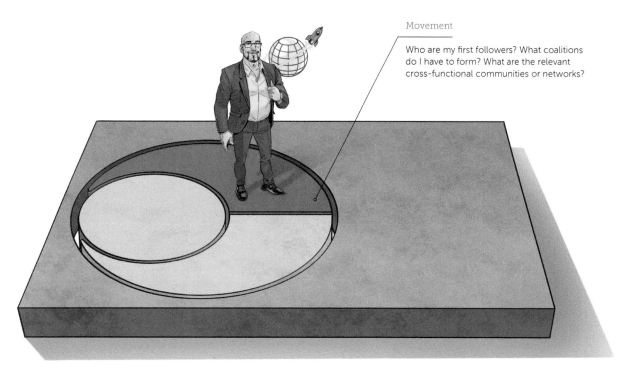

Movement

Who are my first followers? What coalitions do I have to form? What are the relevant cross-functional communities or networks?

Figure 16: Illustration of the Strategy Activation Canvas 2023

Case study: NORD/LB **The #zukunftschaffen coalition**

Sabine Pundsack

Like other banks, NORD/LB was hit by the financial crisis and more specifically by the impact it had on the shipping industry. Following substantial value adjustments in the shipping segment, a previously strong commercial segment of the bank, and the effect that had on the 2018 results, 2019 stood for a year of full of challenges and a new beginning for NORD/LB. The value adjustments in the context of the ship funding portfolio had required capital support, which the previous institutions of the bank together with the Sparkassen Finance Group agreed upon at the end of 2019; it was implemented in December 2019.

The planned capital measures were previously declared free of state subsidies subsequent to an in-depth investigation by the EU Commission. One decisive factor for the positive nod in favor from Brussels was the performance of other, successful commercial areas of the bank in the past. They now constitute the basis for the future business model of NORD/LB. As part of this process, a target vision for NORD/LB was developed together with the old and new owners, to be achieved by 2024. Hence the transformation program launched in 2019 was given the name 'NORD/LB 2024.'

The transformation of NORD/LB involves ambitious target yields. For these targets to be reached, NORD/LB must become more efficient and lean. To be able to take all employees of NORD/LB on the journey and begin with the successful implementation of the NORD/LB 2024 program, a supporting program for strategy activation #zukunftschaffen (#creatingthefuture) was initiated in late 2019. As the project manager, it was vital to me that the transformation not be experienced as a top-down process but be driven from within the organization. It ought to have been clear from the outset that all employees in the NORD/LB Group are part of #zukunftschaffen, not only the responsible project or activation team. For this purpose, we created the #zukunftschaffen coalition: A multiplier network of around 100 colleagues with a special creative drive who had applied for it on their own, thus proving their motivation.

They have shaped and accompanied the transformation of NORD/LB since 2020. Independent of hierarchical and departmental boundaries, they all do their part in taking all their colleagues along on the journey to a successful future. Through their personal credibility, they succeed in making all departments familiar with #zukunft-schaffen and lead them by example. At the same time, they ensure that #zukunft-schaffen remains close to the actual topics and needs of the organization by bringing the impressions they gained in their various networks to the transformation process.

Their initial task was to draw a picture – literally – of the common future and show it to the entire organization. In creative workshops, the #zukunftschaffen coalition members developed the #zukunftschaffen map, a strategy map that addresses the examples of success in the shared history no less than the turmoil caused by the financial crisis. Together with the board and top management, they framed the vision and the shared target vision of NORD/LB. The map shows how customers, employees and the public will experience the new NORD/LB if the strategy is 100% implemented. At the same time, the #zukunftschaffen map highlights the challenges still to be mastered so as to reach a different mindset.

The motto 'From old ways of thinking to a new attitude' is at the center of all activation measures as well. At regular intervals, all employees are going to discuss their role in the transformation program. The #zukunftschaffen members play an

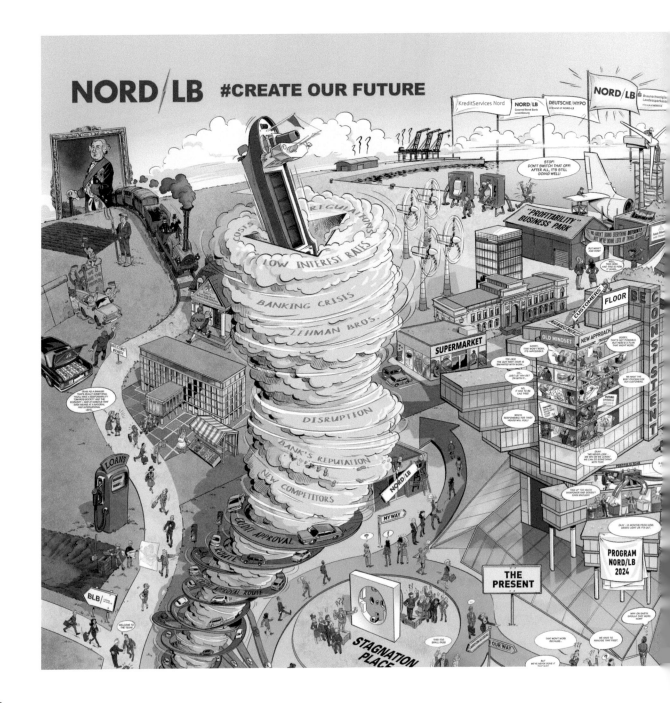

Figure 17:

The Big Picture #Zukunftschaffen

for the N24 transformation program,

NORD/LB 2022

important role in adapting optimally the content of the activation measures to the needs and the current situation of the organization. In co-creation workshops, which, due to the COVID-19 pandemic, have been held online, each activation measure is drawn up and prepared together with the coalition.

Before the results are rolled out to the organization, the #zukunftschaffen members test them for practicability. Acting as a sounding board, they also support the project and/or activation team with assessments of where the colleagues currently stand. They provide their colleagues with ideas of how to keep present the topic of #zukunft-schaffen. Thus they inspire all employees to try out little changes in behavior toward creating the new attitude.

Finally, the #zukunftschaffen members act as supporters and sparring partners for executives, who have to cope with the tasks of transformation on top of their normal leadership work. Whenever possible, they engage in dialogue with managers and board members on how the mutual support may be improved. This does its part for getting open, cross-hierarchical encounters for the common cause.

At the same time, the coalition members actively support and moderate workshops together with executives on the teams or search how the #zukunftschaffen topics can be channeled. In this way, the coalition by word and deed continuously points the way for how all colleagues at NORD/LB can create the future jointly. The coalition is a model for the new mindset prevailing in the entire organization and an indispensable prerequisite for the formation of the #zukunftschaffen project team.

Goals of a coalition

When we refer to a movement, we mean the emergence of social groups across formal team and organizational structures. Movements come into being – sometimes over several years – on the basis of shared themes, values or 'enemies.' There is no or hardly any control from a center. Instead, people with shared interests find one another and form communities that jointly and actively work toward a larger goal.

For strategy activation, a movement is helpful if the shared goal is the corporate strategy and if a great number of employees support it. Since movements can hardly be controlled, we have had great experience with so-called coalitions. They are something like the pre-stage of the movement. Coalitions can be 'forged,' i.e. actively built. At a minimum, one can provide an impetus for a coalition to form proactively along the lines of a shared content frame (of the strategy). The decisive stimulus for the formation of a coalition to activate a strategy came from change management expert Kotter who, some years ago, brought the idea of a second operating system to international business schools and MBA programs.

Kotter's idea: Establish a second network alongside the existing, hierarchical and hence less flexible operating system. In his 'eight step success model' (see Kotter 2018), Kotter recommended populating this second operating system with voluntary representatives from across the company, who are looking for new solutions and ideas of how to drive change in the company and make joint decisions on new strategies and mission statements. Ideally, Kotter says, this second operating system includes 'only' 10% of the workforce.

We want to extrapolate these basic ideas, so we add more dimensions to his idea of voluntariness. More than voluntary, results-oriented and inclusion:

1. Voluntary participants are only one of a total of six coalition options that have proven successful in strategy activation. The composition of the coalition is always determined by the goals of the strategy.

2. A coalition for results should not have 'change' as a goal but only results to be achieved with the new strategy.

3. And most importantly: The coalition is not a parallel system but a movement within existing organizational and team structures.

What exactly should coalitions achieve in strategy activation?

- ✓ Elaborate further the goals of the new strategy and make it more tangible

- ✓ Increase the visibility of the strategy and act as a role model

- ✓ Boost the expertise revolving around the new strategy

- ✓ Strengthen self-initiative and responsibility in the organization with regard to the strategy – the most important goal after establishing visibility and knowledge

- ✓ Keep up motivation and energy for achieving the strategy

- ✓ Energize networking and team spirit

Tasks of a coalition

With these goals, a coalition has four main tasks:

- ✓ **Create attention:** In everything it does, a coalition draws attention to goals to be achieved together.

- ✓ **Clarify the question:** The coalition explains these goals by making them tangible in such a way that everybody understands them and realizes why they're desirable; it conveys that it can hardly wait to see these goals implemented.

- ✓ **Convince:** The coalition reminds people of the organization's strengths (What made us great and successful?) and of the challenges that have been mastered together in the past. It appeals to the strengths of each individual and appreciates the experience of colleagues that may span decades. It asks: How can we make use of all this knowledge, this expertise, to achieve the goals in front of us more quickly?

- ✓ **Point out strengths:** The coalition shows that every employee has done a very good job in the position they were hired for: Customer acquisition in sales; correct calculations in Accounting; winning, promoting and retaining good people in HR; solving problems and offering great services in Customer Support; creative work in Marketing, etc. This means that 95% of daily work is valuable for achieving the strategic goals, and the right focus on the new goals in merely 5% of the daily working hours can make a huge difference for future success.

Types of coalitions

How exactly can coalitions be formed in companies that will increase acceptance and feasibility of strategies?

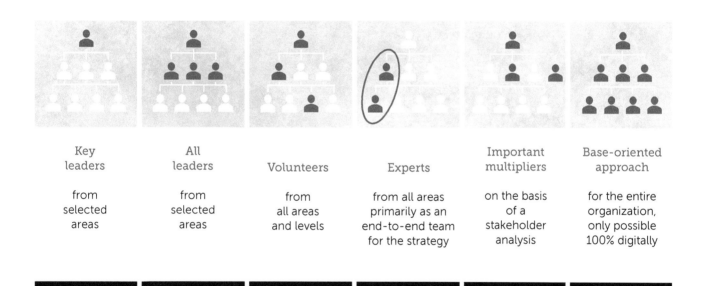

Key leaders	All leaders	Volunteers	Experts	Important multipliers	Base-oriented approach
from selected areas	from selected areas	from all areas and levels	from all areas primarily as an end-to-end team for the strategy	on the basis of a stakeholder analysis	for the entire organization, only possible 100% digitally

Figure 18: The strategic goal itself and the associated new value chain that needs to be built determine the composition of the right coalition for results, TATIN Institute 2023

By forming a coalition, we consistently broaden the basis of people who will commit to achieving the goals set in a coordinated and active way. Depending on the objective, every coalition looks different. In large organizations with several thousand employees, coalitions also differ over time. We have seen the following constellations as successful:

- **Selected key leaders:**
  for instance, while preparing for a takeover

- **All leaders:**
  for example, for enshrining new leadership principles or a mindset change

- **Volunteers from all areas of the organization:**
  for example, in transformation and turnaround programs or when entering a process of transforming the corporate culture

- **End-to-end:**
  for example, in sales strategies or product campaigns that concern only one part of the organization and coalition members are selected along the entire 'value chain of the strategy.'

- **Multipliers:**
  for example, in growth strategies or conquering completely new business models or markets. The most important opinion makers and cheerleaders of an organization are determined based on a stakeholder analysis. Studies show that merely 3% of the workforce can influence the perceived motivation of the entire organization.

If you've found the coalition model that's ideal for your strategy, the next step is to determine the right size. It's worth putting the cart before the horse in this case. What is the coalition supposed to achieve ultimately? How can people in the organization recognize that it was successful? To determine a strong coalition, it helps to look at the tasks it's supposed to assume and the associated key questions:

- **Awareness:**
  Has the coalition succeeded in turning the organization's attention toward the new strategy?

- **Understanding:**
  Was the coalition able to convey the new strategy in such a way that everyone understands where the journey is heading and why they've embarked on it?

- **Preference:**
  Has the coalition found ways for how every person in the organization can define on their own what they personally will contribute toward future success?

- **Action:**
  Has the coalition repeatedly given stimuli for targeted collaboration and action in the spirit of the new strategy?

It's crucial that the coalition has the ambition to set the right framework conditions for the four stages within the organization. It's not about instructions and spelling it all out; instead, guidance is given for contributing one's own ideas and trying things out. And about leeway for controlled experiments. Because while most people are capable of learning, only a few want to be lectured.

Roles of coalition members

The members in the coalition play an active part in strategy activation. We have seen companies, where coalitions were formed that nearly worked as autonomous 'org design units.' Others have set up ambassador programs and equipped them with an proactive mandate and lots of creative freedom. Whatever your coalition looks like, its members will be wearing several hats all at once:

- Multipliers for the new strategy

- Feedback providers for activation team/board/sponsors

- Stimulus providers/ambassadors on teams and at locations regarding the new strategy

- Pioneer and 'tester' for activation measures

- Role models for the new organizational culture: Providing initiative and assumption of responsibility

- Developer of ideas and driver of innovation

- Sparring partner for the board

Thus a coalition acts as a bridge builder between the future and day-to-day operations. So how many bridge builders do you need to activate your organization for a new strategy? Ultimately, everyone must come up with an answer themselves – the example of NORD/LB with 4,500 employees has opened this chapter.

How do you know that you're on the right track?
The movement

If you no longer carry the activation of your strategy forward single-handedly...

■ you will have one (or more) coalitions at your side that can think for themselves and think ahead.

■ you will receive continuous feedback on key issues of the new strategy, which you can consider during the rollout.

■ you'll make consistent use of the experience and knowledge in all areas of your organization.

■ you will have multipliers supporting you who turn words into deeds.

Strategy activation
is not everything.
But without activation,
a strategy is nothing.

Robert Wreschniok

The fields of impact of the Strategy Activation Canvas Putting complexity into context: The narrative and the Big Picture

The third and final element in the 'defining context' field of impact is the telling of an emotional story in an easily accessible and at the same time strong visual language. This completes defining the context. You have clarity about the core of your strategy, a movement in the organization to achieve visibility and effectiveness of the strategy; and now you also have the narrative that doesn't reduce it and simplify it but makes it adhere together as a whole.

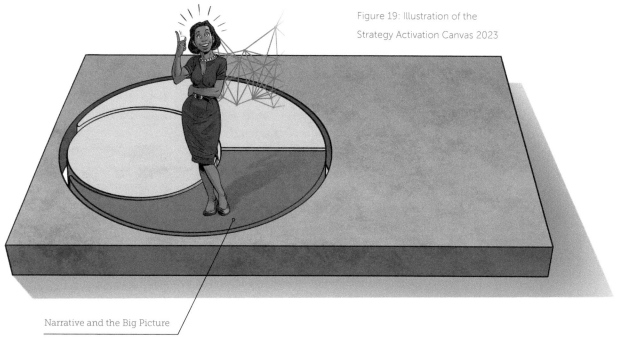

Figure 19: Illustration of the Strategy Activation Canvas 2023

Narrative and the Big Picture

What is the context of our strategy? What emotional and visual story do we want to tell?
How can we appeal to all our senses? What is the visual language? What are the protagonists?

Case study: E.ON **From Big Picture to Big Action**
Interview with Frank Meyer

The energy service provider E.ON has strategically realigned itself – and has entered the direct B2C market with Future Energy Home. With impressive growth figures. The new strategy was established through a Big Picture and activation mechanisms right from the outset – interview with the Senior Vice President B2C Solution Management and Innovation, responsible at the time, and today's CEO of E.ON Italy.

You achieved an impressive boost in sales in your business unit.
What were the decisive levers (retrospectively) for success?
One thing is certain: We were very clear about what we want to achieve from the very beginning: The vision of the so-called Future Energy Home. Everyone is talking about this today, but at the time it was a revolutionary concept. By the way, a concept or term that actually hadn't existed until then and that created a picture in the minds of employees and market participants. In the beginning, we hardly communicated this to the outside because we initially had to prove that the business model would work. This is why we worked a lot with our employees on the energy system of the future. This picture, a clear road map and a focused strategy helped us to achieve great momentum in the company.

You describe your path upon which you started with sales of $20 million
that grew to $800 million inside of four years. How did you create a
completely new business more or less out of thin air?
We had to build a common movement across different countries, which all worked in the same direction. Implementing this through leadership alone is too difficult (seven countries, eleven by now, matrix organization, etc.).

Being responsible for a joint distribution from Italy to Sweden, for instance, isn't simple. We then used a so-called Big Picture (or strategy map as we call it), because it allowed us to tell a thrilling story pictorially: Where do we want to go, where do we detect growth, where are we relevant as market players, what is our reason for existing. Based on this map, we built a team step by step over three to four years and were able to show credibly that we as a team are working together on a plan, have an impact and belong. In alignment with the motto: 'I'm a cog in a large machine and make a specific contribution to success.' Our strategy map was an enormous aid in achieving this goal – what's more, we actually achieved extraordinary results.

**That sounds almost too simple. Do Big Pictures
really only create a sense of belonging?**
You're right – these pictures go far beyond that. Used correctly, they can become a management tool or even establish a leadership culture. Of course, in a first step, the pictures ensure a clear understanding of what it's all about. But the picture also enables you to immerse yourself over and over in the subject matter and work on it (e.g. in performance dialogs held every second week), working on it across different countries and cultures – that has a pronounced influence in the medium term. Again and again, our picture was a starting point for engaging in dialogue, and over time this morphed into an element that linked cultures and constitutes our understanding of leadership today.

**Let's take a closer look at your picture. What are key scenes for you,
and how did you work with the picture as a leadership team?**
For me, the way from the supplier to the solution provider is comparable to a lake you have to cross with speed boats. Boats that were already on the way (i.e. we let them go) but as yet have no idea where they'll land. Or whether they'll sink. To talk about

this uncertainty, to travel at great speed and at the same time to explain in a credible and plausible way that you're moving in the right direction: These are substance-related dialogs you will never get in executive seminars, regardless of how well they are moderated. The exciting thing is that the strategy and the picture are closely interwoven. Quarterly results, business execution, measuring and showing the success month after month – all these things were part of the discussions. At some point, the line between strategy map and actual strategy is blurred. Then you realize that your operational work really contributes to something huge.

**Were there actual moments when you would say: 'They were
critical to success'? Or did success simply materialize at some point?**
Such tipping points actually do exist. One example was that we were able to celebrate success as a team for the first time after two years. We had shown: It is working. Our strategy map has proven itself, and we celebrated together. The fact that you need enough people on such a path who are able to make risky decisions consciously and to break new ground made for another such moment. Certainly, it might have not worked out. But a number of courageous decisions resulted in success again, which we could celebrate. Another proof that our method works.

And thus another shot of courage throughout the company. But don't get me wrong: We did need this time. A strategy map does not shorten the journey you have to make on your own but puts it in a context that you can always refer to. And maybe this in turn triggers decisions that might not otherwise have been taken. And of course there's the moment of break-even. At this late point, we showed: Our target image or picture of the future is a reality.

Figure 20: Big Picture and dialog map for the transforming an energy provider to a provider of energy solutions, E.ON Future Energy Home 2022

Simplification isn't the answer to complexity:

The power of contextualization

Not only are the markets in which we operate complex. Market participants, market dynamics are just as multilayered. The ways of responding to this fact are innumerable. We're talking about the irrationality of decision-makers and about the unforeseen. This mixture of factors constitutes the condition in which we make decisions day after day, usually in accordance with strategies that are sometimes more, sometimes less known to those involved.

And thus it's in the nature of a strategy that it's nearly always abstract. After all, it's meant to establish clarity, simplify, reduce everything to what's essential. Its purpose is to consolidate all available information into probable future scenarios and to deduce from it decisions regarding direction. And that's a good thing. Because this reduction helps to clarify and simplify decisions. Strategies speak to the formal structures of our brain: The memory that collects facts, figures, data, details; or formal operations: Facts depending on persons, locations, times and contexts; i.e. the part of our brain that specializes in 'memorizing' abstract content.

The answer to complexity is context – not simplification.

Ansgar Thiessen

The emotional structure is complementary to the formal structure of our brain.

The part that complements the formal structure of our brain is the emotional structure. Our brain doesn't have to simplify everything. It's perfectly capable of understanding and processing complex nexuses as well as the context. Our experience from many years of strategy work shows: Many employees are seeking this context, the relationships, the conclusions, the cross-references. And the irrationality and the still unresolved issues. Accordingly, we supplement the formal structure of a strategy paper with the emotional structure that doesn't reduce but expands. That illustrates the history of a company in the overall context alongside its culture. Its actors. Its achievements and its darkest sides. Its successes and experiences, which you end up thinking you'd rather not undergo again. And finally a highly emotional target image that doesn't only speak to rational thought but also to joy, pride and self-realization. In short: The contextualization of a strategy.

The answer to complexity isn't always reduction. There's no doubt: Reduction helps to get to the heart of things, e.g. with investors. But it doesn't help to tell a story, one that people can identify with and align their daily work toward. We have seen entire management groups at the medium level facing challenges that are completely watered down in the strategy papers presented.

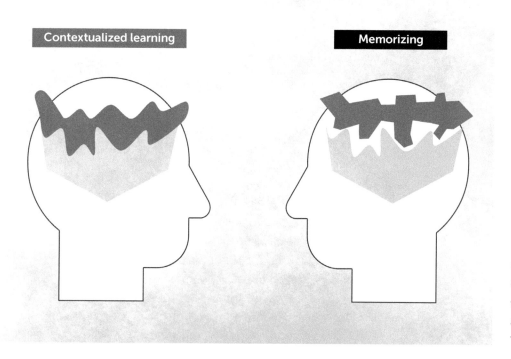

Contextualized learning

Memorizing

Figure 21:
Contextualized learning
versus memorizing
according to Largo 2017,
TATIN Institute 2023

Because it's often up to the managers themselves to reconcile perfectly formulated documents with the daily, living challenges. On top of that, they're expected to become inspired by such abstract papers – very difficult to do, not to speak of passing such inspiration to their teams.

> The emotional realization of the idea of reacting to complexity with contextualization is the drawing of an emotional picture. A so-called 'Big Picture.'

At first glance, it seems absurd to react to complexity with more complexity, because you confuse your own teams this way, right? No. Exactly the opposite is the case – because the presentation of complexity is above all one thing: Honest. Employees are able to deal with complexity and contradictions. Complexity that's well presented helps to highlight correlations. Contextualization is therefore a force that gives employees the opportunity to find their way around. Or to lose their way around and then to keep on searching again for causal relations. This basic attitude of reacting to complexity with context-ualization is fundamental to the idea of drawing the Big Pictures, which we'll describe in detail below.

Drawing the Big Picture: The power of visualization
The emotional realization of the idea of reacting to complexity with contextualization is the drawing of an emotional picture. A so-called 'Big Picture.' In most strategies, communication with symbols dominates when strat-egy must be visualized in the corporate context. The idea behind it: The world, the strategy, our everyday work. Everything is far too complex. We need to be simple again. Simple messages. Simple pictures – then our colleagues will somehow feel involved. Messages must be easily repeatable. Terms and concepts are frequently so unspecific that they might fit any company ('digital first' or 'customer centricity' or 'quality in everything we do', etc.).

Intriguingly, you recognize abstract content with a very simple question: Can you draw it? When you answer this question, you'll quickly find that while we have devel-oped many symbols for abstract terms – a heart for love, a chess figure for strategy, a smiley for joy – these symbols (though drawn) have one thing in common: They don't explain. You don't understand why there is love, whither the strategy is meant to lead or how joy comes about.

Let's illustrate this in tangible terms with the example from actual practice: The merger of two mobile service providers a few years ago. As part of post-merger management, the topic of communication was discussed at great length. The head of Marketing was the lead and presented to the board his 'key visual' for how to communicate the merger. An 'engagement scene' was shown on a poster. A man kneels in front of a woman. Low backlight. The ring at the center of the photograph. The text: 'A once-in-a-lifetime moment' – mobile service providers A and B are going together. The picture was without question professionally done. Highly emotional.

The message was a simple and clear symbol communication and, overall, totally inappropriate for internal communication. Why? It doesn't explain anything. It reduces the merger of two companies to a symbol or an emotion. Things that may well be justified and be effective in product advertising, i.e. in a context, in which individuals can opt for or opt against an offer, spontaneously or consciously but always without force, have a completely different impact in a situation in which a large group of people are confronted with an inevitable and pending or already established reality. The 'once-in-a-lifetime moment' doesn't concern these people, but questions such as 'Which tower will fall?', 'Where will the new HQ be?', 'Who will be the winners and losers of the merger?', 'Why should we actually have more success together?' You see: Strategy isn't simple. It's complex, and people want to know context.

All questions asked are intuitively related to the context in which the merger takes place. And they speak to the much more effective part of our memory, namely the one with narrative structures – the episodic memory that processes experiences and events (spatial, temporal and factual context of memory contents). It's also that part of the memory that will shape massively the 'real' internal communication in the post-merger situation: The table talk with colleagues, the office grapevine; conversations at home or with friends. Stories drive us – not facts. Stories contain facts, but these facts relate to stories as the skeleton relates to the complete human being. Details only make sense in a context. This context and this sense make the details interesting. The narrative contexts are intuitively used by people to add sense to great complexity (like the merger of two companies with many tens of thousands of employees). The question from the point of view of strategy activation is: Can we make use of these mechanisms?

One way to do it is to pay heed to language usage. If leaders and employees articulate their needs with regard to strategy, the greater good that they want to understand is often cited: 'I want to see where the whole thing will lead us.'

> The table talk with colleagues, the office grapevine; conversations at home or with friends. Stories drive us – not facts.

Big Pictures – strategy landscape and storytelling

Drawing Big Pictures brings together two mechanisms that are pivotal in strategy work: First, storytelling, i.e. telling a captivating and simple story; secondly, depth in terms of content and the facts of the strategy.

This is important to understand, because one of the first criticisms of Big Pictures is their 'kindergarten character.'

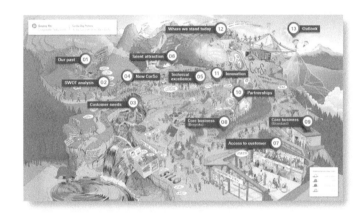

Figure 22: Big Picture of Swiss Re Corporate Solutions (bottom) and the direct reference to the corporate strategy (top), Swiss Re CorSo 2022

However, people who fail to recognize the content embedded in strong strategy papers also fail to recognize the meaning of a Big Picture. Let's take a look at a typical structure of a Big Picture to illustrate this. Broadly speaking, pictures can have three segments:

The history and the WHY of a strategy.
For one, why a new strategy is needed right now and on which assumptions it is based are shown. Secondly, what makes you as a company or team strong; shared experience; projects that went well; as well as things you would not want to do again are pointed out.

The present and the HOW of a strategy.
Here all levers, initiatives and skills are combined that are needed to make the strategy a success. This doesn't necessarily need to refer to skills you already have today. Many Big Pictures we've drawn show desired behaviors, technologies, products, etc., simply everything needed to achieve the strategy.

The future and the WHAT of a strategy.
It may sound banal, but this part is the one that provides the greatest clarity. Because it sums up what's ultimately to be achieved: The new business model in its simplest form, the new clearly-outlined customer segment, etc. A good thing to do in this part of the picture may be to let customers, investors, regulators, employees, etc., have a say. How do they see that the strategy was successful?

By the way, looking back is essential, because most people find it difficult to be motivated by goals they don't understand. And it helps to explain step by step the WHY: WHY do we do that? And WHAT exactly do want to achieve? Combining the two things in one picture makes executives and employees ask themselves intuitively: HOW can I personally contribute to making this story a reality and what are the challenges on the way?

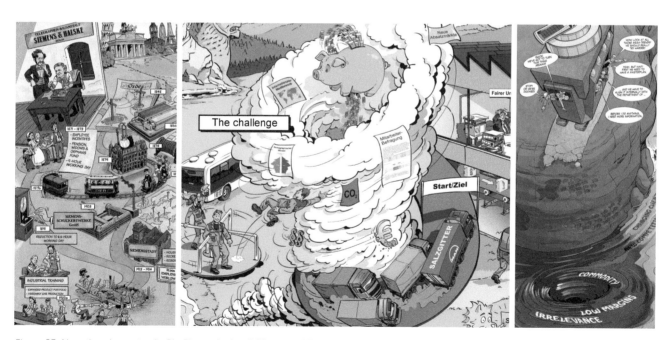

Figure 23: Narrative elements of a Big Picture in detail: 'Our story'; 'The challenge'; 'What will happen if we just keep going like this?' (from left to right), TATIN Institute 2023

A strong source for illustrating graphically the Big Picture is certainly the in-depth interviews in Chapter ➡ Defining the focus: The strategic core. The pictorial language in particular emerges from these interviews: Is it the picture of a theater? Of a racetrack? Of a mountain landscape? Each company has its own pictorial language. Listening carefully in interviews helps to grasp the underlying theme of the picture.

This basic theme is then supplemented by answers to key questions such as....

History

- ✓ What made us strong in the past?

- ✓ What were the issues on which we flopped?

- ✓ What did we learn from it?

- ✓ Have we ever been at a similar point before?

Presence

- ✓ The outside view: What are the major trends in society and in the market that make strategic development indispensable?

- ✓ The inside view: What is our role as a business unit in the group? How are we strategically embedded?

- ✓ Why might we fail?

- ✅ What would happen if we don't change?

- ✅ What are the main priorities on the path toward our goal?

- ✅ Which (entrepreneurial and personal) skills and abilities do we need to develop today that we're still lacking?

Future

- ✅ What is the core of the new strategy?

- ✅ What are the new business models? What are the new market/customer segments?

- ✅ How would we recognize that we have achieved 100% of our goals (customer, employees, investors, etc.)?

- ✅ What does it mean for us as an organization as a whole and our attitude/mindset as individuals?

This basic structure can be expanded as you like, depending on how many segments and scenes you want to incorporate into a Big Picture. Here is an example of a Big Picture, where you can clearly see the three-part structure with a few further partitions:

Experience	Internal challenges	Moments that matter	Vision
What can we build on?	What do we want to improve?	What is important for the strategy to be lived and experienced in day-to-day business?	What will it be like when we have achieved our goals?
Negative scenario	**External influences**	**Key initiatives**	**Monitoring**
What happens if we do not change anything?	What do we have to accept?	How can we pool our resources to improve our competitive position?	How do we measure if we are on the right track?

Figure 24a: Subject canon of a Big Picture, TATIN Institute 2023

What's decisive here is that every scene, every tiny detail has a reference to content. A reference primarily to the overall strategy and then to the sales strategy, HR strategy, customer segmentation – in short: To all vital concepts of corporate management that are in place. At the same time, the pictorial representations refer to projects, the corporate culture, desired behavior, etc. Nothing is left to chance; the entire visual language is reflected in data, facts and analyzes. And that's exactly what makes the picture so powerful: It's a pictorial narrative (storytelling) of the why, the how and the what of a strategy (strategy map).

Figure 24b:
Big Picture of a digital transformation. Agility is not a question of technology but of the mindset, TATIN Institute 2023

Internalization of strategic content

So now we have a Big Picture – but honestly, what do I have with it? Let's look at the mechanism from the perspective of organizational learning.

Above all, Big Pictures achieve a considerably improved chance that the strategy actually reaches our colleagues and is understood by them. If a strategy is presented by PowerPoint, for instance, only 20% of the content on average is remembered. Active engagement with a visualized Big Picture results in a ratio of up to 90% of internalized strategic content.

Moreover, the Big Picture creates a kind of 'knowledge on hand,' available to everybody, and thus results in binding rules in terms of behavior in everyday work. It relieves all those involved from the torture of having to learn by heart and rattle off increasingly meaningless core messages; but it allows everybody to tell the same story about the organization's future in their own words, along vivid, tangible scenes. This way, different interpretations are prevented.

Big Pictures help all those involved in a strategy not to solidify meaningless core messages any longer through repetition but to bring them to life instead.

And: Every employee recognizes himself or herself in various scenes, can develop self-reference and clarify his own contribution to the Big Picture. A special drawing style allows for representing critical elements, concerns and challenges such that they result in broad acceptance and prevent past mistakes from being repeated.

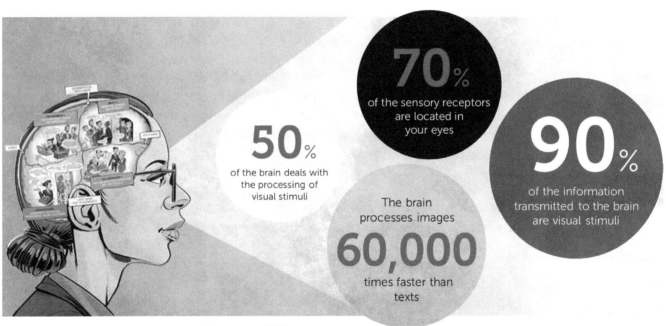

Figure 25: Impact of visual communication, TATIN Institute 2023

A Big Picture can be used as a central activation platform to accompany and accelerate a transformation process all the way up to successful implementation.

A one-of-a-kind and distinctive tool: The comic book style is quite different from normal corporate or advertising graphics. It's catchy and allows for conveying even difficult topics (e.g. staff reduction) or emotional content (e.g. new ways of working) effectively and appreciatively. What's decisive for maximum activation effect is that the recipients see something new and unusual. In this way, we can increase the cognitive enshrinement of strategic content in their heads from 20% (PowerPoint) to about 75%-90%.

More than just facts: Stories matter more to people than just facts and figures. Unlike pure infographics, the illustration style can capture and trigger emotions that have a particularly strong impact on preferences & behavior. The pictorial style also allows for making compelling connections between individual scenes to be experienced.

Address & resolve issues honestly: To achieve the activation of employees and their engagement with strategic content, it's pivotal to visualize even those things that aren't yet working properly. The applied style of illustration creates a communication platform where it's easier for leaders to talk about weaknesses or unresolved issues. At the same time, the style helps employees identify the issues and increases the acceptance of the strategy through self-confident transparency.

Strategy cards are based on the principles of STORYTELLING: Where do we come from? What made us successful? Where will the journey take us? How is our path toward the realization of our goals different? How will we and our customers recognize and experience success? By telling an exciting story, strategy cards offer a tangible answer to the ubiquitous problem of complexity – not by simplifying but by conveying the overall context.

'Moments that matter' approach: One last important methodical lever for strategy activation consists of translating abstract numbers that are based on future-oriented strategies to so-called 'Moments that matter' (see also Chapter ➜ Focus on moments, not on figures in this playbook). By this we mean the moments in the daily work experience of an employee that might have a huge impact on future success right at this moment. Big Pictures arrange these moments into a storyline, creating a knowledge on hand for the colleagues who are involved to get to the largest common success lever in daily implementation of the strategy later. Our brain processes pictures 60,000 times faster than text.

Visually prepared content is accessed 94% more often on the Internet than content without pictures. The memory of visual strategic key content is heightened by up to 75%. And still, strategy is delivered in a PowerPoint presentation by 98%. Big Pictures show: This need not be.

How do you know that you're on the right track?
<mark>The narrative and the Big Picture</mark>

If you tell the strategy as an exciting story about the future
of your organization during strategy activation, then...

- you provide an answer to the question of complexity through context, not bullet points.

- everybody will talk about the same Big Picture in their own words.

- you'll see yourself, your team and the overall idea at a glance.

- you'll realize that identity arises from the past, the present and the future.

- you'll detect even critical topics and challenges to discuss and recall them.

- the strategy will turn into knowledge on hand in the form of an exciting
  visual story and not into another dead PowerPoint corpse.

- you'll share with all colleagues a consistent, shared and coherent target image.

- the things you want to achieve together will be clear to all,
  so they want to get started right away.

The fields of impact of the Strategy Activation Canvas Accelerate strategy and transformation processes

In the Strategy Activation Canvas, we now take a step away from the 'defining context' field of impact to the part of the activation mechanisms. While the elements discussed so far are something like basic work, the following elements are used primarily in the work in the organization: systematic listening, where the challenges for the strategy lie; focusing on a few central topics that are important for the strategy; establishing behavioral changes in the organization and much more. All this is done in the context of the strategic core, with the help of the movement along the narrative that we have developed up to this point.

Activation

How can we listen systematically? What do we need to draw attention to? Where do we want to try out new things? How do we create sustainable activation? How do we measure success?

Figure 26: Illustration of the Strategy Activation Canvas 2023

	Strategy as a campaign ('prescribe')	Strategy as activation ('appreciate')
Target group	**Selected groups:** E.g. management, selected leaders	**All:** without exception
Employees	**Consumers** with the assumption that they align their daily work to the strategy	**Active promoters:** with the certainty that they align their daily work to the strategy
Scaling approach	**Top-down presentation:** through existing hierarchies	**Co-creation of content:** Across the boundaries of functions, regions and even hierarchy levels
Procedure	**Cascade:** From management to the lower levels of hierarchy	**Invite:** In work groups that are important for specific activations, always with the aim of reaching everyone
Understanding the dialog	**Dialog as an event:** Through dialog workshops, their documentation and final report to the board/management team	**Dialog as a source:** I.e. consistently starting with the results of dialogs and constant development of content
Communication	**Tagging:** Typically one-way communication that wants to nail down (core) messages	**Contextualization:** showing contexts and leaving enough leeway for own interpretations
Formats (selection)	**Campaign:** E.g. Town-hall meetings, newsletters, emails, executive blogs/vlogs	**Dialog:** E.g. dialog sessions, challenges, micro experiments, blended learning, working out loud
Integrating existing initiatives	**Align:** with ample leeway for interpretation	**Embed:** with a clear bearing to the strategy
Personal contribution	Is largely left to the employees **themselves** (typically developed and prescribed by middle management)	Is created and developed clearly and **unambiguously** by the teams and employees themselves
Level of meaning	**Words:** Gathering behind consensus terms (digitization, customer orientation, innovation, etc.), which are then rubber-stamped	**Meaning:** Clear awareness of the specific things one can achieve oneself and how to contribute actively to the strategy
Target focus	**Change:** Focus on perceived weaknesses and shortcomings that keep us from achieving goals	**Results:** Focus on the experience, strengths and skills of employees that help achieve goals
Basis for action	**Announcements:** prescribed or at least pre-thought instructions for action	**Guiding principles:** provide the framework in which behaviors and actions are developed and thought through independently

But what actually is activation? The decisive – but not the only – difference between change initiatives, culture initiatives and transformation initiatives, as most of us know them, and activation is the full involvement of employees. This means no longer seeing employees as consumers but as active promoters of a strategy. Promoters who ultimately write the narrative themselves (and not only the communications department). Promoters who develop the skills and experience they need on their own (and not just the HR department).

Promoters who define the focus of what's important (and not just managers). Etc. But there are more differences between strategy as a campaign and strategy as activation – two perspectives that aren't mutually exclusive but complementary:

This chapter is dedicated to selected tools and mechanisms of activation. We have made a conscious selection here. In the end it's not really important which tool you choose for activation. We have seen the best ideas coming from the teams themselves anyway. The compilation should be seen as the offer of a modular system, for leaders, strategists and organization developers who initiate an activation.

We concentrate, as it were, on those tools that have been tried and tested many times, that lead to clear results and are pragmatic in their application. The compilation is based on a logical sequence: First I have to listen, then define a focus before I can experiment; what works well, I can run permanently and measure. This sequence is not the last word, on the contrary: Depending on where activation is at the moment, mechanisms can be selected and combined.

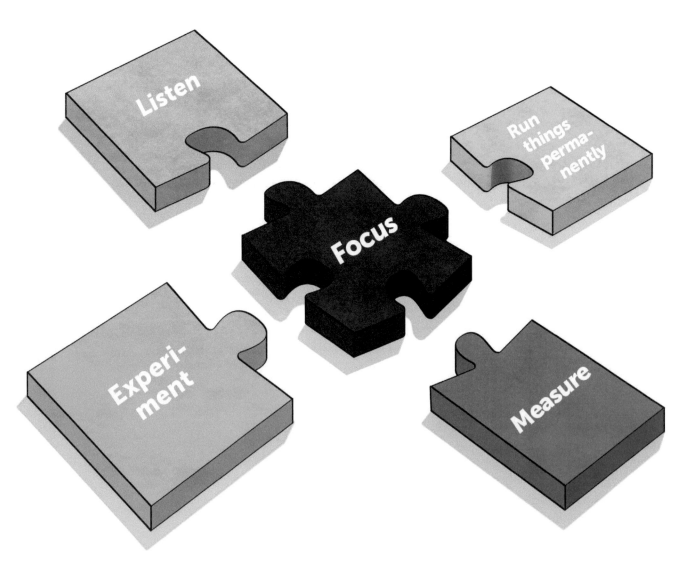

Figure 27: The 5 mechanisms of strategy activation, Strategy Activation Canvas 2023

Listen

Successful strategy activations start with honest listening: Which parts of our strategy are actually understood? Where do our employees see the greatest strengths of our products or our culture? What are these permanent failures so that we make such slow progress with our strategy? As described at the beginning (see Chapter ➲ Understand the core: A look behind the strategy paper in this playbook), these questions are an excellent source for accurately identifying the issues and moments that stand in the way of strategies or might greatly accelerate them.

But listening requires brutally honest reflection, something most executives don't do and don't want to do. We experienced time and again that surveys, for instance, were interpreted beyond recognition, for the simple reason that the result cast a poor light on department heads, division heads, etc. This is why the first part of strategy activation is about listening precisely to what is actually happening all across the organization. We saw that corporate culture is often driven by criticism. Employees love to articulate why something cannot work instead of saying how it might work. You can use this fact to activate change. Because let's be honest: If people tell me about their concerns, it's something like a Fort Knox of experience.

What we mean by this is: Concerns, collected and evaluated centrally, can be quite valuable for the architecture of activation mechanisms. Either because the concerns point to real challenges. Or else because you realize that a section of the workforce is not yet mentally behind the new target image. Both things help to make a transformation more successful in the end. Because the human brain is fundamentally a defense machine. For evolutionary reasons, anything new is seen as risky. Or else interpreted positively. It's worthy of questioning. So whenever you read or hear something new, the brain automatically compares it with what you've already experienced, read or learned. And at points, where the new thing contradicts your experience, the brain says: Yes, but....

Mechanisms of listening should always be about establishing ways of making use of this apparent negativity. Basically, an organizational dialogue is built:

Figure 28: The human brain as a 'defense machine' against topics

1. I'll give you a new strategy.

2. You provide me with your experience ('Yes, but...').

3. These 'Yes, but...' comments are systematized...

4. ...and an 'ear' is planted in the organization (coalition for results).

5. With digital means, this interplay of listening and activation can then be made permanent as a continuous process in the entire organization, e.g. by introducing personas that assume different perspectives of the strategy; see ➲ The example of Gaby Go (open to new things), Will Wait (skeptical about new things) und Dr. No (wants to prevent anything new) later in this Chapter.

In short: Skepticism, saying no, criticism, etc., should not always be seen as negative; they can actually be systematized and embedded in the activation: Gold nuggets and excellent sources that underscore those aspects vital for a successful strategy activation. Let's take a look at the mechanisms of listening.

This mechanism is certainly one of the most exciting and requires a little bit of courage: Inquiring consciously and explicitly about hurdles and stumbling blocks for a strategy. To illustrate this with an example, we had the CEO present a new growth strategy at a major company event: He tells a rousing story, supported by strong arguments and plausible figures, data and facts. Everyone believed that everybody in the room was allowed to ask questions at the end of the presentation and then go back to their desks.

> The conscious and explicit inquiry of hurdles and stumbling blocks for a strategy is a source of activation mechanisms.

However, we turned the tables during this event and had the CEO ask those present: 'Why do you think that this strategy won't work?' With this simple question, we systematically identified the weaknesses of the strategy by having everybody work in small groups all through the room. Without having to employ consultants for weeks, because the expertise was present with those people who deal with the products and services day-in and day-out. After the question was answered, we had the groups work on another one: 'What are your ideas on removing these hurdles you just wrote down within three weeks?'

Again, we bundled together the extant knowledge into valuable content. The analysis of the two questions was extensive. Subsequently, all the items that blocked a successful strategy implementation were analyzed by project teams. There is no way that we would have this information from the company more precisely and, above all, more quickly. The nudge theory provides similar examples. In meetings concerning the solution of a problem, the exact opposite is done: The problem is framed in more extreme terms. The mechanism is known as 'flip-flop.' For example, if the issue is the improvement of customer service, the meeting starts with collecting ideas on how to lose most of one's customers in a very short time. The exciting thing is: The results for the solution (improving customer service) are significantly better after this simple exercise (see Eppler & Kernbach 2018).

Another mechanism for the successful activation of strategies is making use of negativity: 'It aims at something that every one of us knows: The 'Yes, but...' response. Will the new product campaign work? 'Yes, but...' should we as an insurance company bear the risk? 'Yes, but...' do you really believe what the CEO just presented? 'Yes, but...' Not only do we know this reaction only too well – it is actually deeply rooted in the very way we function as human beings.

The human brain is trained to deal with new information skeptically and cautiously. The reason for this goes back to prehistoric times when our very survival was at stake. Every new piece of information, every new situation could end in death. And this natural reaction drives our subconscious to this very day. That's fair enough because any strategy, realignment or reorganization may have tangible consequences for my own job. So I look at it critically and with a little distance: 'Yes, but...'.

Negativity as a source for strategic stumbling blocks[5]

'Making use of negativity' doesn't refer to a policy on how to prevent the 'Yes, but...'. Instead it means understanding the 'Yes, but...' coming from each individual as something positive: As 'gold nuggets' in every process of strategy activation. Every 'Yes, but...' that is expressed provided direct and condensed feedback that conveys the entire work experience of the person saying it. And a description of what — based on experience and knowledge — might actually become an implementation obstacle for the new strategy.

What matters most: To integrate the 'Yes, but...' answers effectively in the strategy implementation work, they must be systematically collected. 'Systematically' refers to the selection of the people being interviewed. They should represent the entire impact chain of the new strategy. Secondly, the comparative analysis of the answers should be done in a structured way. Because individual concerns are interesting and may be correct but aren't necessarily so.

If the analysis of the collected 'Yes, but...' answers shows that 80% of the interviewees, for instance, point to the same problems, it would be reckless to ignore them for strategy implementation. On the contrary: Successful strategy activation starts with the deficits collectively perceived in an organization. In other words: How can we organize the situations pointed out (e.g. 'We are uncoordinated in our budget process because we work 100% in silos') that they lay the cornerstone at this early point in time for successful goal attainment and avoid insular solutions and change requests?

Is it time-consuming? Not necessarily: Take the example of a CEO who presents his new corporate strategy in a large town-hall meeting to the entire team. For about half an hour he talks passionately about what will occur on the markets over the next few years and what role the company will play in it. We all expected that he would end his plea with 'I'm inviting you to get involved' or 'If you have any questions, we'll send you a PDF of the PowerPoint by e-mail'. Far from it: He addresses the assembled executives: 'Now tell me why the strategy won't work.' Then all managers are divided into groups of 5 and are asked in a first step of individual reflection to name the three top reasons for the strategy to fail. The results are then presented per team and weighted. Subsequently two teams go through the same process and so forth.

One and a half hours are enough to collect strong content about the stumbling blocks of the strategy. Something that they would have had to find out in tedious interviews going over months; or even something that would only have come to light the moment people realize it's not actually working. In the end, the top activation hurdles are prioritized.

There also is a psychological effect that again uses the basic mechanisms of how our brain works: When the speakers of the teams presented their results, a 'Yes, but...' effect could be observed in the statements made. Instead of: 'I find the strategy impressive, but...,' you now have sentences along the line of: 'We see the three biggest hurdles here but believe we can get that under control by....' Now the CEO has his management team exactly where he wants it to be: In the middle of a lively discussion about how the new strategy might actually work.

Another example of exploiting 'Yes, but...' for strategy activation is the coalition for results. The coalition brings together colleagues along the entire value chain of a new strategy and from all areas and hierarchical levels. The goal is to identify possible implementation hurdles for a strategy before it's rolled out. When a new sales

> And now tell me why the strategy won't work.

strategy was launched in the enterprise division of a leading mobile service provider, for instance, various scenarios related to the new strategy were played out using story-telling methods in a group consisting of sales employees, product developers, call-center employees, colleagues from Research and Development, Market Research as well as customers.

Among other things, the question was posed: 'Imagine sitting down with colleagues in three years' time. The mood is as much at rock bottom as the figures; the new strategy hasn't worked. Why did it fail?' The decisive factor in this approach is that individual opinions about the negative development are initially collected separately, then combined again and grouped together. This ensures that all perspectives of the various teams are included and have been understood. Of course, here again the point is to design ideas for activation in accordance with the relevance and frequency of the pitfalls in implementation (see also Fischer & Wetzel 2015).

These examples demonstrate how important it is not to label immediately negative comments and hints as the opinions of grumblers and old-school adherents. To see them instead as information on where the planned strategy may have stumbling blocks and then eliminate these obstacles in a targeted way. The speed of the implementation can be increased many times over than having them learn something arduously during the journey.

Figure 29: Using resistance and different perspectives as accelerators of strategy activation, according to the Theory of Constraints (TOC), Eliya Goldratt, TATIN Institute 2023

Turn resistance into accelerators

77% of employees say that there is no open handling of critical issues in their company (cf. HR- Report 2015/2016 Schwerpunkt Unternehmenskultur,' Hays 2016, p. 14).

> Not only the promoters but also procrastinators (factual reservations) and skeptics (personal reservations) belong to the group of colleagues that help you to translate your strategy into practice.

When it comes to advancing new strategies, concepts and goals, everybody likely has had the painful experience of having worked on and fine-tuned the strategy for many weeks and months; and all they get for their efforts are misgivings and 'Yes, but...' arguments. 77% of all employees who have had poor experience with how critical issues are dealt with at their company show that you are not alone in this experience.

And so does the study 'Theory of Constraints (TOC)' by Dr. Eliyahu Goldratt (cf. Techt 2010). Along the axis of factual objections and personal reservations in the corporate context, all you can hope for is 5% of promoters. But expect 40% of skeptics, 40% of procrastinators and 15% of active resisters. And that prior even to having started with your strategy.

If you believe brain researchers, this seems to be an evolutionary trait: Be cautious, don't trust every new person immediately, listen to their personal experience. This is called 'healthy skepticism' in the everyday language, and because it sits deep in the human brain, the phenomenon is global and can be seen in the corporate culture of European, Asian, North and South American companies.

The one aspect that differs greatly according to culture is an openness to show and utter such criticism and skepticism. From the point of view of strategy activation, this evolutionary secret contains a 'gold nugget of activation' and the acceleration of strategy and transformation processes. The theory of constraints can be included in the storytelling of the Big Picture – we demonstrate it by using the example of three personas, a resistor, a promoter and a skeptic/procrastinator.

**Will Wait or
Marc Wait a Moment**
He sees the glass as half empty and is skeptical about new things, either for personal or factual reasons.

**Gaby Go or
Jana Now**
She sees the glass as half full and is open to new things.

**Dr. No or
Dr. Nope**
He sees the glass as neither half empty nor half full. He doesn't want any water at all and is against it in principle.

Figure 30:

Example for interviews with the personas

of activation in an employee magazine, NORD/LB 2022

From the perspective of strategy activation, we view reservations and 'Yes, but...' objections and concerns arising from them as extremely condensed, completely free and focused work and life experience. As to how it works is what you are experiencing just now when reading this book or talking about it later. Whenever we are confronted with a new thought, our brain works in the background without us being aware of it and compares the new thought with things we've already experienced. Every time something new encounters something already experienced, a concern, an objection, a reservation are expressed. Something contradicts our personal or factual experience, and therefore I disagree.

And at this moment, skeptics and promoters turn into accelerators of my strategy implementation because they immediately supply relevant information on activation barriers, i.e. breaking points in my strategic considerations. Does this necessarily mean that the strategy is bad? Does the strategy have to be written anew? We don't think so. For activating the strategy, it's extremely helpful to include any barriers in your considerations.

The most important aspect when using concerns and reservations in strategy activation is that it be done systematically. Knowing the concerns of one colleague is interesting. But collecting the concerns of the 30 colleagues, whom you think essential for the success of the strategy, is productive. Not every factual or personal experience is decisive. But if 24 of 30 people point to specific barriers, it would be criminal not to include it in the calculation from the onset. This is how it can be done step by step:

> The most important aspect when using concerns and reservations in strategy activation is that it be done systematically.

1. In a first step, it helps to ascertain the collective experience, thus the concerns and objections in the organization. This can be done, for example, in in-depth interviews (see in detail in Chapter ➲ Defining the focus: The strategic core) with the key stakeholders for the strategy implementation or in live interventions with selected leaders. One way to do this is to have senior management present the strategy and then have teams of five to eight work out why the strategy will not work in any case as planned.

By setting the task and by working as a team, you ensure that everybody has the opportunity to express concerns and reservations. You'll be surprised when the concerns are presented to learn that some teams of skeptics will immediately and without being asked present solutions on how to deal with the obstacles. Again, our brain does what it has to do: As soon as we hear a problem, the solution machine fires up.

2. The second step consists of forming a coalition from the ranks of promoters, skeptics and procrastinators (see in detail in Chapter ➲ Form a coalition for results: The movement).

3. The third step is about involving the resisters in the activation process. Unlike skeptics and procrastinators, resisters are not interested in a solution. They disapprove. Period. On principle and without seeing any need to justify it. Although at 15% they are a minority in the company, they can have a negative impact on the overall mood, which then also drags down those with a basically positive attitude and puts the entire process at risk.

How to deal with the resisters? According to our experience, it works best when they are given a voice.

From town-hall meeting to 2-week challenge

Most company town-hall meetings we have seen follow a very similar basic pattern: CEO and CFO present key elements of the ongoing strategy as well as the underlying key figures. Depending on the focus topic, other leaders then present the current status and, if applicable, the next steps. Q & A are often determined with the aid of online tools and unanswered questions are answered subsequently on the intranet. Back to the desk.

There is nothing wrong with this form of communication as such, especially if we're talking about events for pointing the way forward. After all, they convey in condensed form knowledge relevant to a broad audience. But you need to know what this type of town-hall meeting ultimately is: A presentation, listening, hardly any resonance as to how strongly the things presented will be remembered.

Let's look at this from the perspective of science. The so-called activation pyramid shows what percentage of the content lands in the heads of the target group according to the method of transfer. When we place town-hall meetings as we know them in this pyramid, you can clearly see that they are in the passive part of the pyramid.

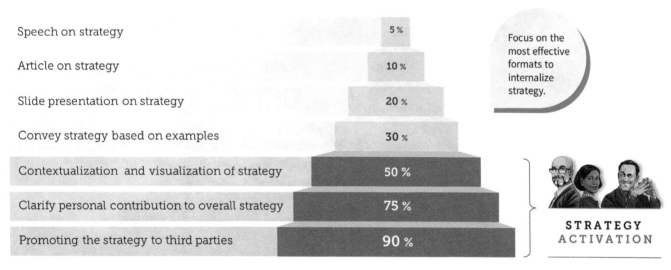

Speech on strategy — 5 %

Article on strategy — 10 %

Slide presentation on strategy — 20 %

Convey strategy based on examples — 30 %

Contextualization and visualization of strategy — 50 %

Clarify personal contribution to overall strategy — 75 %

Promoting the strategy to third parties — 90 %

Focus on the most effective formats to internalize strategy.

STRATEGY ACTIVATION

Figure 31: Memorizing rate of strategic content along carrier media, shown as an activation pyramid, TATIN Institute 2023

This means that town-hall meetings are usually formats of strategy communication, not strategy activation. In a nutshell: Only 5% of the content of a strategy lecture will stick in the memory of the audience. Even PowerPoint presentations with memorable visual elements and examples from actual practice only reach around 30% of listeners. And the obligatory Q&A session after the lecture is not really a group discussion either!

From the point of view of strategy activation, we see an exciting phenomenon here: In a well-run and successful company today, there will be only a few areas left in which most of the time (and most of the money) is knowingly invested in processes that have proven to have the least impact, to put it bluntly. Town-hall meetings can be combined and expanded with other formats at will.

An example from our actual work practice:

The town-hall meeting was great. The strategy presentation was greeted with huge applause. There were only a few questions. So: All seems to be OK. The mood during the day and evening is great, and even the daily online survey showed: 8 out of 10 would recommend the event. And yet: The pay-off came 3 months later in the annual commitment survey: 85% 'miss a strategy.' And the result included both employees and managers.... Are town-hall meetings an expensive and stupid idea? To answer the question, we ought to remember once again what these large-scale events on strategy activation are actually meant to achieve. There are four main reasons for organizing an in-person or virtual meeting with a large number of employees:

> Town-hall meetings can be combined and expanded with other formats at will.

1. to influence/persuade others;

2. to come to decisions;

3. to solve problems together; or

4. to strengthen relationships.

All these goals are active processes, but as we have seen in the learning pyramid, town-hall meetings are not in the active area. The key question is not: How can we communicate the strategic content?

But: How do we ensure that up to 90% of the strategic content is absorbed by the people in the target group such that it leads to active, targeted and sustainable action? This makes it clear: Large-scale events can do more than just present content: They are moments of listening and participating.

Town-hall meetings as a 'pit stop'

One example of this was the work with around 200 leaders of a company with almost 3000 employees, who opted for the format of the 'Big Picture' to present their strategy (see Chapter ➤ Putting complexity in context: The narrative and the Big Picture in this playbook). We deliberately left some areas empty for the completion of the picture. Specifically those that describe how customers, employees and other key stakeholders would experience success.

We had the leaders develop this content digitally; after all, they are best suited to assume this perspective owing to their many years of experience. And again, we were able to use the content 1:1 to complete the Big Picture as well as to determine the focus that is most important for successful strategy implementation.

Town-hall meetings as interaction

Another example, again from a town-hall meeting, is working with digital tools (such as Pigeonhole) that enable direct interaction (up to controlling the course of a large-scale event). It isn't uncommon in town-hall meetings that questions get asked by individuals.

Or they are digitally supported (e.g. www.slido-com), which allows for a certain ranking. But digital tools can do much more: Have topics determined right from the start that are most relevant to employees ('live polls'); conduct surveys in between; find out key areas ('heat maps' or 'word clouds') or provide data and have it interpreted ('real-time reports').

The example of our town-hall meeting had to do with the inclusion of so-called word clouds, in which participants can enter one or two terms relating to one question (e.g. 'What's the most powerful feature of our business unit at the moment?'). These terms are then visualized based on the frequency by which they were mentioned: More mentions move the term to the center, where it is shown bigger than other terms. In our example, the managers in the room could then initially react to it live and continue to work with the result later.

Figure 32: Wordcloud to query mood images in live meetings, TATIN Institute 2023

Town-hall meetings as the beginning of a 2-week challenge

Our last example is to use the town-hall meeting as a kick-off for a so-called '2-week challenge.' Such a challenge has the entire organization work on a specific task for two weeks right after the event. This may be the solution to problems; rationalizing of content that was presented; sometimes even the development of content ahead of a major event. We are familiar with similar forms from Kaizen or lean Six Sigma, where solutions are found with all necessary experts; the 2-week challenge expands the time period and refers specifically to the content of a large-scale event.

One example of such a challenge is retelling a strategic story once the CEO has presented it in a town-hall meeting for the first time. Typically, people just download the presented slides after the event; some continue to work with them; others go back to their normal day-to-day working. After the presentation of the story, all employees can be invited to tell the story themselves to 7 to 10 colleagues as part of the 2-week challenge. And have the narration accompanied by a couple of questions (e.g. 'Which parts of the story do you find easy to tell?' or 'In which areas of the strategy do you think we're not ready yet?', etc.). The results from these questions are then summarized online in one place and turned into valuable input for where the strategy should be further honed and where other solutions should be applied directly.

The advantage of the challenge is that everybody is involved. Thus the impact of a large-scale event is getting much greater resonance in the organization. Furthermore, the presented content does not disappear immediately after the event, but resounds clearly, sometimes causing chain reactions of further events, discussions, solutions, etc. Finally, challenges can be used to collect content on a broad basis, similar to the formats of listening. The character of a challenge lends to the whole affair a playful, almost competitive character. At the end of the challenge, not only can everybody in the company use the Big Picture to relate the strategy as a thrilling story about the future of their own company, every person understands the context as well and is able to name moments/scenes in the Big Picture where they can make the greatest contribution to future success. Now they all can start to focus on results and common goals.

These few examples show that major events and town-hall meetings can do far more than elucidating PowerPoint slides, listening to a handful of speakers and answering poorly presented questions. Intervening like that in an organization is of limited value: There is hardly any certainty about what has been understood and what it triggered in the organization. In the worst case, everything swings back to the existing routine. A limited number of mechanisms can help to generate content, define a focus, direct the course of an event toward relevance for the participants and lots more. It requires some courage on the part of those on stage (whether leaders or moderators) to respond well to unforeseen events.

How do you know that you're on the right track? `Listen`

Once you have gone from being a loudspeaker
to being a listener in strategy activation, then...

- you'll begin to see 'Yes, but...' and concerns as valuable experience
  and knowledge that help you get ahead faster because you use them
  become better,

- you'll no longer be hoarse from presenting the same
  PowerPoint for the perceived 1000th time,

- you can suddenly hear how colleagues talk about the company's
  future instead of always saying: 'We have no strategy!'

- colleagues will tell you how they shared the exciting story
  about the future of their company with family and friends.

- you'll notice that organizations don't follow some theoretical change
  curve but that colleagues are sometimes in the past in their heads,
  sometimes in the present time and sometimes in the future. You can
  transform 'talk past one another' into 'talk to one another' and

- you'll find that there's a Gaby Go, a Will Wait and sometime
  even a Dr. No in yourself, depending on the topic and the mood.

Focus

The next aspect of activating mechanisms is about the fact you don't have to change everything in the organization to implement strategies successfully. On the contrary: Normally, just a few selected areas, persons, projects or even moments will suffice for the wanted impact or change to go into force. Annual slogans, must-wins, iteration visions – all these are mechanisms we know from traditional management theory that basically aim at exactly the same thing: Separating the noise from the signal and, wherever possible, driving forward only those matters that visibly contribute to a strategy. In the following, we present four focusing mechanisms.

Focus on goals, not change

One of the biggest barriers to activation for accelerating strategy and transformation processes is due to a confusion of means and ends. The purpose of any implementation of a strategy or transformation is to achieve their goals. Therefore the focus should be on this purpose from the very beginning. A change program is often established as the preferred means:

> One of the biggest barriers to activation in accelerating strategy and transformation processes is due to a confusion of means and ends.

A program management office orchestrates all the measures necessary for achieving the transformation. The risk here: The change becomes the goal, and achieving the actual goal falls behind. It's no longer economic growth that is measured but how many managers attended a training event, what is reported to the steering committee at what time, etc. The means conceals the purpose and leads to frustration, resistance and delay.

With the installation of change programs comes the question, often raised in work-shops, of the change of employees and teams: 'How do you need to change today to achieve our new goals in the future?' This leads to two issues: First, people don't like to hear that they need to change. Secondly, the question implies that everything that people have done so far or what they are today is no longer sufficient. An image of man based on the lack of something.

What can be an alternative to change programs and the demand that individuals change? We base our image of man on abundance: 'Imagine the strategy you are pursuing will be 100% successful in 5 years' time.' Now the crucial question: 'You're responsible for strategy, you know the market like no one else does, you graduated from the top university. How would you use your knowledge, your skills and experi-ence to achieve this goal as quickly as possible?'

That has a completely different vibe, right? So we suggest: Focus on the depth and richness of individuals in strategy and transformation processes and invite them to shape the change with all their knowledge, skills, expertise, etc. Let's take a look at three types of employees to see how this approach works with them:

The old hand

You've been with the company for nearly 30 years. You've witnessed and helped shape the grand era and also did your share during difficult times. You know from decades of experience what is feasible and what has already resulted in failure. How can you contribute your knowledge and experience to help us achieve this goal more quickly?

The rookie

You just arrived from the university. You've been with us as a trainee for four weeks. You know our market as somebody who makes a decision for or against our offer. What is important? Why didn't you grab it? When would you do it, and what would you do first so that we achieve our goals more quickly?

The expert from the (enemy) office next door

You know everything about IT and you know the advantages and limits of our infrastructure better than most. With regard to strategy, what do you think we absolutely need to pay heed to and what would you do about the highest hurdles that stand in our way so we can achieve our goals more quickly?

All of a sudden, the change and the individual's need to change were no longer in the foreground but, instead, the privilege to make a contribution so the commonly defined goals can be achieved.

Figure 33: Illustration of three personas with different experience, TATIN Institute 2023

Focus on sprints, not a marathon

We would like to describe this focus by way of an example. The enterprise division of a global leader in mobile communication needed a mindset change from a quantitative one to a qualitative sales approach. For decades, the sales team for corporate accounts was trained (and incentivized) to sell as many SIM cards as possible to corporate customers. The sales department was very good at this, better than many others on the market.

At this point, the market is saturated and 100% quantitative growth is hitting its limits. The natural consequence: Sales figures stagnate, a call for a radical rethink is heard: Accusations are thrown around. 'You've lost your touch.' 'You're resting on your past laurels.' 'We need new people.' 'We must have a mindset change.' 'We must radically question everything.' 'Change course!' Etc.

Luckily for the sales department, none of this happened. Today it is again one of the most successful in the market. Instead, thought was given to the question of how the sales figures can reach their old glory again. If you can't sell more cards, how can we generate more revenue per card? It will no longer be possible with mobile phones. So completely new products and services were developed. A new qualitative sales approach evolved. At the same time, the 95% to 5% rule applied during the entire process:

95%: What did everyday work look like in sales with the old, quantitative sales approach? There was far too much bureaucracy. Appointments were made. Customers were visited for sales discussions that lasted 40 minutes on average. Trade fairs and roadshows were prepared and done. Presentations were given there, networks were built and contracts were concluded.

5%: Training for quantitative offerings. Exchange of ideas, experience on how SIM cards can be sold to companies. What works, what doesn't work any more? How can it work nonetheless? What arguments are strong at the moment?

The difference in activation was that the colleagues from sales were now faced with the question of changing only 5% of the 100% of their job. They pondered: What actually made us the best sales team on the market? Why did we have such strong sales despite far too much bureaucracy? How did we succeed in acquiring the most attractive customers? How did we build a world-class network on the market? The results of these deliberations were then deployed: How can we make use of all that to be as successful in the new 5% of our job? Today, the sales department mainly sells services – far more than the 5% they started with.

What we want to demonstrate here: In transformation processes, you win over employees by focusing on small changes and exploiting the existing experience. Appreciation of what already exists and then transferring it to the new thing is more effective than questioning everything and giving the impression that everything people are accustomed to must be radically changed.

Focus on moments, not figures[6]

So-called 'moments that matter' (or 'moments, of truth or 'key moments') is another way to focus. This refers to moments or levers in the day-to-day work of a leader or employee, which are demonstrably those relevant for achieving a target image successfully (see Heath & Heath 2017). Let's take a look at an example that shows how difficult it actually is to identify such moments (see, for the most part, Thiessen & Wreschniok 2019).

In transformation processes, you'll win over employees by focusing on small changes.

'To start with the good news: A perceived 98% of the day-to-day work will remain the same following a transformation. Here is an example from the aviation industry: In the newly outlined strategy of a global aircraft manufacturer, 98% of the daily routine of a pilot will not change in his own perception. The alarm clock rings at 5:30 in the morning. Cold shower. Getting to the airport and the plane.

Coordination with the crew and ground personnel. Checking the engines, etc. The same is true of the daily routine of other groups of the staff: Check-in, back office and, yes, management, which begins in the morning, coffee at hand, in front of a computer sorting through emails and warming up for the daily meeting marathon. And yet it is the few moments, for instance when the pilot goes to the bathroom, in which he must adjust his previous way of acting to ensure 100% safety for the flight (see Thiessen & Wreschniok 2019).

'Moments that matter' do not postulate the need for a fundamental change program that feigns transformation when there is none but, instead, directs the extremely scarce resource of 'attention' to the few moments, which – with regard to the new strategy: – yield significant added value in the day-to-day work right now: What kind of behavior can be used to convey maximum safety in the new discount airline? How can we find new ways to work together more effectively in the established company? What are the moments during which new, agile methods of management make sense, and where are they counterproductive? When does the 'either – or' dogma apply, and when should a 'both – and' mindset guide decision making?

The 'moments that matter' approach doesn't look inward but forward. It doesn't ask how we need to change but which moments in day-to-day work already have the greatest impact on future strategic success. And: What can each individual do right at that moment to achieve visibly better results? Specific everyday situations as levers for strategy activation, i.e. moments that matter, have another vital advantage: They not only make strategies visible and tangible – they involve employees directly. The situations that contribute to implementing the strategy are rarely board meetings or management offsites.

On the contrary: They are established meetings, situations for decision-making or voting and coordination, sometimes employee interviews; they may occur during the onboarding of new employees, one moment during check-in – in short, very specific situations in the day-to-day work of employees.

If you use moments that matter, abstract strategy papers become a part of tangible, everyday actions, and everybody involved in them sees what their contribution to the overall strategic success is.

Another example: The moment that resulted in the improvement of customer orientation in the IT department of a global investment bank. The bank's board triggered an unprecedented momentum from the day it praised individual employees for their gracious conduct toward customers in monthly telephone calls with roughly 50 participants. A single phone call every four weeks, a few minutes (and thorough preparation of the board members) are required to show something as abstract as 'customer orientation' in an understandable way to top executives. Not less but also not more – and the board has achieved something several previous change projects couldn't do nearly as well: A longing for being more customer-oriented (see Thiessen & Wreschniok 2019).

Moments that matter ...

- are quite specific moments in day-to-day work (i.e. not abstract situations such as 'meetings' but something like 'the moment I pick up the phone when a customer calls')

- address the future (i.e. not any future but the future that is described in concrete terms in the company strategy)

Focus on strengths, not weaknesses

Some of the most impressive studies on the subject of the mindset are undoubtedly those by Carol Dweck, who differentiates between a 'fixed' mindset and a 'growth' mindset. Her work has become the basis of leadership development or organizational development in many places (the case study of Microsoft in this book is based on Dweck's assumptions). The difference between the two mindsets is the mental perspective on things: While a fixed mindset assumes that abilities are innate and difficult to change, people who think in a growth-oriented way assume that everything can be learned. With far-reaching consequences in terms of challenges, problems and everything that ultimately needs to be overcome.

> While a fixed mindset assumes that abilities are innate and difficult to change, people who think in a growth-oriented way assume that everything can be learned.

Figure 34: Illustration of super-powers as part of a strategy activation project, TATIN Institute 2023

195

The idea of the growth mindset was further developed by the California-based transformation consultants SY Partners (who, among others, saw Starbucks and Facebook through transformation processes). They argue that every one of us has a set of 'superpowers' besides their professional skills and experience: skills that define each individual and that combined are valuable for strategy work. Again the focus is not only on the professional background but on personal talents – another activation mechanism.

Below is a selection of these superpowers that have been further developed by the TATIN Institute for Strategy Activation and that we use in activation.

What is your superpower?

Energy
Individuals with lots of energy are true motivators and can easily electrify the people around them. They don't take themselves too seriously and know exactly how to create the right mood. They keep their teams on track and succeed in motivating their teams when people start feeling exausted. They come closer to their own goals as well as exhibit a high level of efficiency because they are able to convert energy into focus and concentration.

Sometimes too much energy looks like impatience and may result in the team's concern of not being given enough leeway. Although a good mood can help to resolve tensions, it may distract from problems and be perceived as inappropriate.

Empathy

People with the 'empathy' superpower have a finely honed sense of the needs of other people around them. The gift of being able to hear what's unspoken enables them to grasp the emotional state of their team intuitively. In conversations, they easily find the right words and hit the right tone. All this makes empathetic people excellent mediators in building relationships. With their remarkable perceptual ability, they get beyond the facade of their colleagues and become familiar with all their peculiarities.

With too much empathy, colleagues may have a hard time seeing the empathetic person's own standpoint since they look at the world only from the perpective of others. People with a lot of empathy sometimes help others to perceive their own emotions clearly. Then you must take time to discuss the emotions.

Problem solving

Problem solvers zealously get to the core of a problem and fix it in no time. With just the right questions, they find out where the problem lies and why it exists, thus pointing to solutions that were hidden up till then. While others get cold feet, they get into gear in earnest when problems crop up. Therefore people with this superpower can be of great help to their team when it hits a dead end.

They work fast, even in stressful situations, and may always be a few steps ahead of their team. With too much problem-soving power, colleagues might struggle to keep up, so breaks are necessary.

Provocation

For them playing safe doesn't exist. This superpower provides people with a layer of thick skin and lots of willpower. Provocateurs regularly push the team out of their comfort zone and thus discover hidden potential. They're not content with mediocre accomplishments and always strive for perfection. The team needs them if it lacks originality.

Too much provocation is often seen as unpleasant criticism or even as insulting, thus trust is lost among the colleagues on the team. This trust is the precondition for colleagues to be receptive to the provocations in the first place.

Eagerness to try out new things

People eager to try out something new are always full of ideas. They're able to develop various strategies in a flash, implement the most auspicious ones and fine-tune them along the way. If the team gets stuck, they can help and provide the right kick in the butt. Fear of failure is unknown to them.

Too much eagerness to experiment may have an intimidating impact on others since not everyone feels comfortable with such speed in the work mode. So it may be necessary for colleagues to divide things into smaller portions and approach the goal step by step, lowering the risk.

System thinking

People who think in systems help the team navigate and weigh the pros and cons. System thinkers aren't afraid of the unknown. When others can no longer see the forest for of the trees, they keep a perspective on things. When problems crop up, they work systematically and bring all the threads together since they're able to see the connections between apparently unrelated factors.

Too much system thinking can be problematic if a decision on the team has already been made. This superpower makes you review things time and again, which can be grueling for other people. Too much of this superpower may also confuse colleagues, especially if they're involved in all the details. They can't see what people with system thinking see.

Striving for harmony

People with a strong desire for harmony try to minimize conflict. They have a good sense of recognizing the strengths and weaknesses of colleagues and then connecting them in the best possible way, based on what they have in common. This way they give a team that is still a bit wobbly on its feet a common path.

Too much striving for harmony. Sometimes minor conflicts are necessary to move forward. Then co-workers who strive for harmony should hold themselves back somewhat so as not to stand in the way of optimizing the team.

Simplification

People with the 'simplification' superpower work through a thicket of information and tasks, when everybody else has lost track and steamroll past every barrier to get to the next step. If the team is confronted with a mountain of results and isn't sure what they all mean, people with this superpower can help find the recurrent theme.

Too much simplification can lead to colleagues being left behind because they don't have enough time to discern the light at the end of the tunnel on their own. What is needed here is patience. Moreover, it is vital in stress situations not to omit details, so that others can follow.

Decisivenss

This superpower gives people courage to make decisions and stand by them. With ease and self-confidence, they weigh the pros and cons, break them down and make a decision. They pursue a pragmatic instead of a perfectionist approach, since they are aware of the plethora of possibilities and know that there is nothing like the only true one. They quickly come to conclusions – yet not at all recklessly or impulsively. They just have developed a formula over time that combines sophisticated analysis, experience and great instinct.

In stress situations, too much decisiveness may cause colleagues to feel pushed upon. Especially when a decision is postponed over and over again, decisive people easily get impatient.

Stamina

People with pronounced stamina are the driving force on the team in a long-distance race. With their motivation and perseverance, they carry their teammates along on the track and push them over the finish line. They drive things forward until they are done and distinguish themselves by a high level of tenacity and focus.

Too much stamina can cause other colleagues to be left behind on the exhausting track because they don't have the same endurance. Breaks for the entire team are essential.

Negotiating power

For people with negotiating power, negotiating is an art they practice with great passion. Their precise judgment doesn't let them down even in difficult disputes or disagreements. They're assertive yet willing to compromise, which makes them quite valuable to the team.

Too much negotiating power sometimes has an intimidating effect on other people because not everybody feels as comfortable negotiating as those people with this superpower. And there might be some team members who bring a lot of emotions to the process and take things too personally.

Recalibration

If the team has lost its way a bit and the emotions are running high, a colleague with the superpower of recalibration can help. Such people are immune to disturbances from the outside and always manage to bring the situation under control. They are clear-headed and focused and don't get worked up over anything.

Too much recalibration is sometimes repulsive to emotional colleagues since they don't see calm and equilibrium there but indifference. It may have a frustrating effect, because it seems people with this superpower aren't supporting the team.

How do you know that you're on the right track? `Focus`

Once you've gone from the abstract to the concrete in strategy activation, then...

- the shared goals before you will become more important than the collective navel-gazing about how we supposedly have to change.

- you'll feel how you can make a difference every day with your work, not only by participating in change programs.

- colleagues all of a sudden join in because they know how to contribute their strengths.

- you'll know the moments in your daily work that have the greatest lever for future success.

- the oftentimes invoked transformation will take place all on its own because everybody thinks about what they contribute to the new and how new things evolve through the exchange of ideas.

Experiment

A narrative that is readily and frequently used to spread a spirit of optimism and confidence is the idea of being a 'pioneer.' It is a wonderful metaphor indeed, but its true strength is rarely told. In customary change narratives, the pioneer metaphor focuses on the idea of 'being first.' First on the moon, first on the mountain top, first in a new world. Of course that is one aspect that characterizes a pioneer. Another important feature is the following: Pioneers fail many times before they reach the goal. Pioneers don't give up. Pioneers try out new paths if the first ones don't work out.

Pioneers aren't admired but are, at most, mocked. Pioneers persevere for a long, difficult time before they reach their goal. It also may be a pioneer's story never to reach the original goal; but, instead, to find another one on the way there that turns out to be all the more valuable. The pioneer metaphor is not a crude 'We want to be the first and the best' story but an excellent narrative about agile working, thinking in options, expecting no thanks for trying out something new but glory if it works.

When it comes to activating organizations, all these supposedly dark sides of being a pioneer (all the things happening prior to the glory) come to light. The positive handling of them is often referred to as error culture in business contexts. Anybody who has understood the concept has no problem with it and can see the acceleration force behind it. But anyone – particularly in the German-speaking regions – who is confronted with the concept as part of a new transformation program as the new 'slogan from the boss' is completely baffled. Focusing on mistakes?

Making mistakes to learn from them? It sounds wrong, and that is how it's understood. This is why we have been looking for new words and ended up with 'trial and error culture.' Trying out something new. Using tiny steps. Controlled experiments and pilots, which are rolled out step by step, are tested, sometimes discarded, sometimes improved but always tried out in actual practice as early as possible.

For autonomous teams to complement one another mutually in their activities, to think and work across departments, a common narrative is needed, as introduced in Chapter ➡ Big Pictures – strategy landscape & story telling. There are dozens of narratives, none of them completely wrong or 100% true; what counts is to find the metaphors for the narrative that relate the strategy as an exciting story about the organization's future. Using the example of the popular pioneer metaphor, we want to provide some clues as to what must be paid attention to.

How do I get an organization to experiment?
The first challenge when systematically involving as many colleagues as possible is to find the right balance. Trying to get ideas from 10,000 people for the implementation of the strategy and trying them out in a first step is a fascinating but naive thought – in reality, it amounts to a real nightmare. 10,000 ideas have to be reviewed, evaluated and, usually, rejected.

The great participation turns into a great collective disappointment. And many ideas can't be tried out just like that. They require precise preparation, planning and budgeting; a project office for implementation and both financial and human resources. In short: They don't want that.

There are a number of pragmatic mechanisms and levers when it comes to activating the organization both on a large scale and in a controlled manner. It's important to....

- ✓ focus on those moments in the organization that promise to be the strongest levers for future success; in many cases, this may be things that simply contribute to the improvement of operational excellence (see Chapter ➡ Focusing in this playbook).

- ✓ to align the organization along 'processes that guide thoughts' so as to 'try out new things,' channel them sensibly, for example with the 'Circle of Influence' concept or the 'Tiny Habits' defined by the University of Stanford.

- ✓ facilitate 'trying out' in controlled experiments with subtle methods such as nudging or systemic approaches, e.g. 'Working Out Loud'.

Let's take a closer look at these levers.

Processes that direct thoughts

Figure 35:
Circle of Concern &
Circle of Influence
according Covey 1989

After having described the 'moments that matter' in the 'Focusing' chapter, we now would like to present the 'Circle of Influence.' The basic idea is to concentrate in your daily work as well as in your personal thoughts on things that can really be influenced. To separate them from topics that someone will very likely solve but that you cannot impact personally ('Circle of Concern'). The following example illustrates this idea:

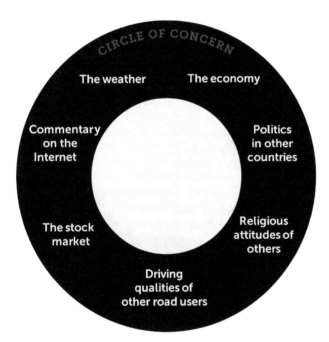
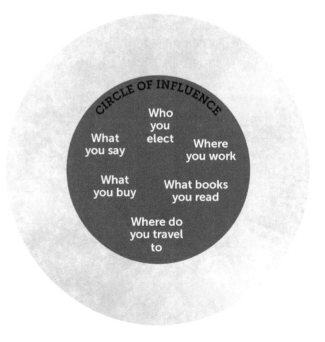

When it comes to establishing a culture of trial and error within the company that helps to achieve strategic goals more quickly without overloading the system, you should direct your thoughts toward the Circle of Influence.

Because employees who understand what's at stake since they know the Big Picture and have identified the moments in which they have the greatest personal leverage for future success and are aware of their strengths – if they work on these very moments, the Circle of Influence hands them a powerful method to develop genuine self-efficacy.

Even simple training events or workshops with teams on the Circle of Influence versus the Circle of Concern are useful for employees to learn focusing radically on the things they can personally solve. We have seen that a lot of people try to blame other teams or other people when it comes to developing solutions. You want to escape this trap. An exercise about your very personal Circle of Influence is enormously helpful for making things happen.

> The Circle of Influence hands a powerful method to develop genuine self-efficacy to employees who understand the Big Picture.

Tiny Habits

Another strong method regarding the Circle of Influence was developed at Stanford University called 'Tiny Habits' (see https://tinyhabits.com). The idea behind it: If you want to change (corporate) culture in the long term, don't start with big new values or even bigger change programs – start with many thousands of new Tiny Habits.

How does it work? It begins by becoming aware of daily routines. It's a 'tiny' start: Every morning, my feet touch the floor when I get up. Every day I brush my teeth, meet people, consume media, eat, go out with people; I talk, engage in dialog, go to bed.

The goal here is to link selected tiny rituals with new habits, which in turn contribute to personal or, if you like, strategic goals. Goal: I want to feel better. Every day when my feet touch the floor for the first time (ritual), I'll say: Today will be a good day (new habit). Goal: I want to lose weight. Every time the waiter offers me bread in a restaurant (ritual), I'll say: No thanks (new habit). Goal: More focus at work.

Every time I start my computer (ritual), I'll switch off my social media notifications (new habit). Goal: Improved cross-functional collaboration. Every time I start a new project that sooner or later will affect the adjacent department, I'll invite one of the colleagues there to a kick-off meeting.

Making these Tiny Habits accessible and comparable to colleagues, anonymously or with your own name, brings an exciting element to the activation of organizations. These habits can evolve with respect to corporate values, new (agile) work processes or the attainment of new strategic goals. Again what is important here is to define the process accurately and holding back on the 'how'. As soon as you start to dictate to third parties their Tiny Habits, you have just invented micromanagement on the social level in the company, and what you get is the opposite of activation. An aphorism: The hardest thing is to find is order in your own life. The only thing that's even harder is not to impose this order on others.

Working Out Loud (WOL)

The method of Working Out Loud doesn't really have anything to do with loud work. It's well-nigh a culture-defining method: participating in small groups (so-called 'circles') in the professional and personal development of the others (see in particular Bryce Williams 2010 and John Stepper 2015 and/or https://youtu.be/XpjNl3Z10uc).

In principle, WOL is goal-oriented development, growing together, a generous sharing of knowledge, cultivating new relationships and making one's own work visible – in other words, for the most part a peer-learning process.

> The hardest thing is to find an order for one's own life. The only thing that's even harder is not to impose this order on others.

In Working Out Loud, three to five employees meet together at regular intervals (usually one hour per week) over 12 weeks. Participants come from different areas of the organization to talk about their professional and personal development. Because these circles meet regularly, participants support one another in achieving the goals set at the onset. Working Out Loud uses various agile mechanisms: Cross-functional participants, self-organization, retrospectives and dealing with critical feedback.

The procedure is pre-structured but also designed to be very free. In the first session, the circle defines a shared learning goal or topic that they would like to deal with (see the so-called 'Circle Guides' online at https://workingoutloud.com). After that, the self-organized work begins. Using the method's five principles, participants share knowledge, think about how to get nearer to their learning goal, make their own knowledge visible. Being curious and acquiring knowledge, pursuing a shared learning goal incidentally establishes new networks and relationships, which didn't exist before since attendees usually didn't know one another up to that time.

What are we trying to say here? Working Out Loud is a method of experimenting with knowledge, developing solutions together, penetrating topics, all in a fairly free and appreciative atmosphere. Some companies now have thousands of WOL circles, including BMW, Bosch, Deutsche Telekom and Siemens.

Trying out things systematically and in a controlled way

Let's take a look at all the mechanisms we have discussed up till now: Contemplating the personal moments that provide the biggest lever for future success, one's own strengths, Circle of Influence and individual Tiny Habits as well as discussing these things in WOL circles are all excellent opportunities to activate ideas and topics relating to a strategy or transformation. But how do we get from self-reflection to collective and coordinated action?

Here the idea behind WOL can be further developed and applied directly to strategy activation – effectively as a 'process to guide thinking' without giving up the freedom of the method. Over the 12 weeks a circle lasts, there is an agenda for every two weeks:

1st week
Communicate context. The Big Picture approach is used for the strategy.
Ideally visualized; the teams discuss this context.

2nd week
Establish self-reference. Where do I see myself in the Big Picture?
What are my strengths that I can bring to bear?

3rd week
Discover required capabilities in yourself: What am I good at today
that I can contribute to the activation of the strategy?

4th week
Approach real challenges quickly in the solution mode. Where are we stuck?
How can we make things happen in our Circle of Influence?

5th week
Consolidate or begin with a new topic?

6th week
We use the R-factor learned from the pandemic for our own purposes.
At least two team members agree to set up their WOL team, and within
a few weeks, the entire organization is activated.

This cycle can be cultivated in independently acting teams to become a perpetual motion machine of strategic success, perhaps starting in one's own department and then spreading across divisions.

The time required for such a procedure is based on the knowledge that little time is left in a jam-packed daily schedule. 24 minutes a week suffices for a mission meeting. Structural changes: What we discuss and try out does not add another to-do to the list that is already too long; through the Circle of Influence, we focus on things we already do and learn how to implement them more quickly, better, more correctly and with more fun – not only on one's own but on the team.

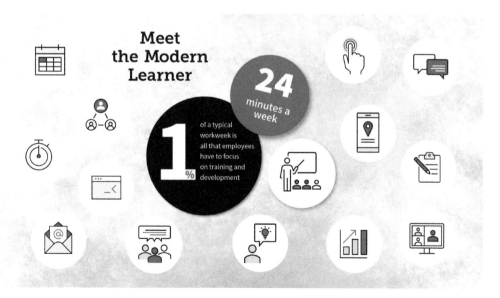

Figure 36:
Meet the Modern Learner
according Bersin by
Deloitte's 2014

Tiny Interventions

One of the most powerful activation mechanisms to constantly drive elements of the strategy forward, are so called 'tiny interventions'. Before we introduce the mechanism, let's spend a moment on one of the most prevalent challenges you face with any intervention in organizations: Time. Or better, the perceived low value of the intervention against the day job, which almost always ranks higher when it comes to setting priorities in the daily agenda. Now, whenever you as leader or organizational developer are seeking for perceivably additional 'burden' to the daily work – be it trainings, activation interventions or change interventions of any kind – the reaction you hear the most is 'we don't have time for this'. Or, if for example the participation in trainings is being measured, you will most probably hear 'let's get it over with as fast as we can, so that we can return to our day job'.

24 minutes each week

One way to overcome this challenge is to introduce small or tiny interventions. Which means, that you break-down a large amount of time needed to build capabilities, to e.g., rationalize elements of your strategy, or to foster activation dialogues, or to train knowledge, etc. down to the minimum amount of time needed, which is a) bearable and b) enough so that learning sticks. Which is in fact 24 minutes per week. The foundation for this idea comes from the Bersin by Deloitte study (see Figure 36) showing that 1% is what an average member of an organization is willing to invest or is, in fact, realistically available, if time is not set aside to deliberately for learning. You could argue that 24 minutes is neither enough to drive topics nor does it sustain knowledge, dialogue, activation of any kind. Even more so, such small interventions seem more to be one-shot-wonders. The trick is that you perform the interventions week by week (no exception) and you craft an architecture for a multitude of interventions.

TINY INTERVENTION

TEAM SKILLS

AGILITY

HIGH PERFOR-MANCE

PSYCHO-LOGICAL SAFETY

FEED-BACK CULTURE

TODAY

1 YEAR LATER

Figure 37: Only 1% of your working time invested in strategy oriented team development create massive effect over time, DAY7/TATIN 2023

Meaning that you provide your team-leaders or management teams with a set of interventions, crafted along the topics you want to activate, and from which leaders then can individually pick and choose. Depending on the topic they themselves want to drive forward or value the most.

The example of this German luxury car manufacturer charmingly shows, how it is providing a bouquet of tiny interventions to their global leadership, which is relevant to their 2030 strategy. In the form of an online library of interventions, managers themselves decide which ones to take to their teams at any given point in time.

Steering with facts
Each intervention the car manufacturer measures in term of completion, empowerment created, impact identified, collaboration increased etc., which allows to continuously evolve the content and type of intervention. As a result, the library grows and becomes more precise and valuable to global leadership with every release.

Tiny interventions as part of existing meeting setup
Going even one step further, organizations we have seen, that drive an architecture of tiny interventions, often integrate them into their existing meetings. As a vast majority of leaders do spend a huge amount of their available time – in meetings. Be it team meetings, project steering bodies, brainstorming sessions, one-on-ones, and the list goes on. As during an hour of a weekly team meeting for example, carving-out 24 minutes and dedicate them to strategy is far easier than scheduling another 24 (or typically 30) minutes into an anyhow packed weekly agenda. However, both approaches (integrated and dedicated) work – as long as the intervention time set aside is scheduled for week after week after week.

Figure 38: Each Tiny Intervention can be used intuitively, without preparation and during existing team meetings, Day7, TATIN 2023

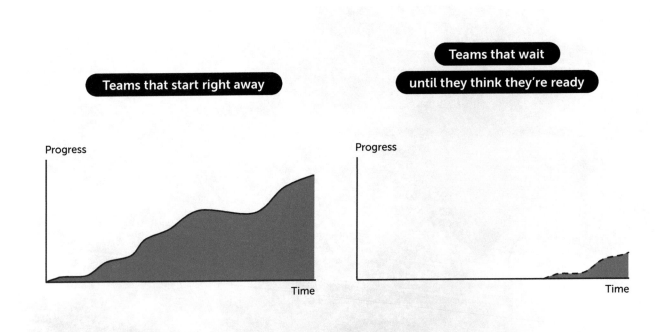

Figure 39: The early start allows significantly faster results, DAY7/TATIN 2023

Almost infinite possibilities

The library of topics for tiny interventions can be huge: From specific topics towards your strategy (e.g. with a direct link to your ➡ Big Pictures – strategy landscape and story telling) to a vast number of more broader topics, such as

- participative leadership
- small successes towards Big Picture
- learning from mistakes
- showing sincere interest in employees
- work as reflective tasks
- goal setting

Pretty much any topic, that drives your strategic or leadership agenda (the examples shown above address for example psychological safety, as to Edmondson, Goller/Laufer or Ditert/Trevino). You may even celebrate the completion of all tiny interventions within e.g. 12 months with a certificate – which may then be either a prerequisite of a leadership program or simply to proudly share on internal or external social media.

Micro Experiments

The last method we're presenting we have seen in a perfected state at Google and Amazon: The systematic performance of so-called micro experiments. That means: Try out, try out, try out. At times, have teams compete and move on only with the best solution.

When performing large-scale experiments, two things are crucial: First, end experiments. We have seen companies that start one pilot after another without ending any of them, thus increasing complexity instead of reducing it. Secondly, analyze experiments systematically. This means that not the experiment is important but what we've learned from it: What worked and why; what didn't work and why; where is it worthwhile to continue the experiment, where is it not? What knowledge may not help me but will help somebody else.

This is the only way to scale knowledge and transfer it to many areas of a company. Courage to declare the failure of experiments; share what we have learned with others without having to be asked; these are mechanisms we have seen in companies that have made experimenting the core of their culture of ideas.

How do you know that you're on the right track?

Once you've gone from talking to doing in strategy activation, then...

- you'll focus on those points you can actually influence in your day-to-day work.

- you'll discuss those items with your team that can be improved not by an individual but by the organization, because you all want to work in a place that makes it easy for you to succeed.

- you'll find out how different views of one and the same topic can enhance your own perspective.

- you'll have found ways to develop further on the team and become more efficient and effective in your work because improvement happens 'on the go.'

Run things permanently

Strategy activation is not a project that starts at some time and then ends. Because even if the implementation of the strategy has been accomplished at some point, there will be a new picture of the future, new markets to conquer, new technologies to develop, etc. And even if a strategy isn't successful, the moment will come where assumptions will be questioned and a fresh target image will be defined.

Thus the activation of strategies means reflecting upon and negotiating the future and defining what contribution the overall organization can make to this picture of the future. In our experience, agile mechanisms are particularly helpful in keeping strategy activation running in the long term. Because they provide the organization with a 'heartbeat' that continues to produce and deliver. Synchronized autonomy means that human beings take center stage, so that they can contribute their capabilities to the Big Picture.

So activating strategies is a constant reflection and negotiation about the future.

There are certainly other ways to lend a permanent momentum to activations. In the following, we will present only those mechanisms from the agile toolbox with which we've had a positive experience. Before we enter into each of these mechanisms, a word about what we don't mean by agility: The launch of agile setups (e.g. the Spotify model, the SAFe Framework, the scrum methodology, etc.).

What we propose is to harness agile mechanisms and principles and translate them into pragmatic solutions and setups. Accordingly, we structured the following chapter on the basis of key agile principles and demonstrate how they can be used for the work of strategy activation.

Case study: Allianz **#lead – What makes a great leader?**

Interview with Tony White

# #

lead is a global initiative of Allianz as part of its transformation program that aims at providing all leaders with a capability development environment that does not so much convey content as demand concrete dialog for visible change. #lead is provided on a digital acceleration platform where roughly 18,000 leaders work on so-called 'missions.'

Let's begin with something quite basic: What are the requirements today and in the near future for the development of leadership capabilities at global corporations such as Allianz?

Clearly two things: The personification of learning and the provision of relevant content in a timely way. Let me explain. The most obvious answer to the question of requirements would be the buzzword digitization. But that's not true – I hardly know of any corporation that has not created a digital learning and development environment. But only a few of them have succeeded in making this environment effective. When we talk to our learning professionals, we frequently hear that the learning content is far too general.

They address large groups of employees, not however individuals who want or need to grow in a specific field. This is what I mean by personalization. It's only possible if we offer not only our own content but also freely available content on the Internet or the semi-available content from many universities or learning providers, all of which make their content accessible to the public nowadays (best-known example is probably Harvard University).

Secondly, it's important to make personal learning content available precisely when it's needed. By the way, digital learning is only a part of the range: Learning from others (again, made available in a personalized and timely way) is something many corporations have just begun systematically to use for themselves.

That's interesting. What do you mean by 'learning from others'?
How can I use that?

Look, today you can connect to and network with any inspiring leader. You simply write an email or watch interviews on YouTube. Thus you can advance your own leadership style, even if the leader you have listened to doesn't care about the values or beliefs of your own company. That's the challenge: Psychological studies show that you normally follow people who have a similar way of thinking as yourself. But does that really help you develop? This is the risk we have in learning today: That we live in echo chambers with people who learn the same things as we do, thus limiting even more our own learning and thinking.

And how to tackle this risk?

For us at Allianz, we think bigger when it comes to learning and capability development. We investigate the question: How can we help employees create the right environment for themselves, so they can learn and grow from a future perspective? There are many jobs in industry today that are being automated and replaced by artificial intelligence (AI). We, too, will be sitting next to an AI one day, and therefore we have to feel comfortable with it. Learning and leadership must contribute to the training of our employees, offering them an environment where they can grow or re-qualify to meet the requirements of this new future. This is the only way to shape the future and not be overrun by it.

How to you develop leadership capabilities at Allianz?

You know, the worst level of online and e-learning platforms is where you learn with the mindset of 'If I don't do that I won't be compliant and have practically one foot in jail.' Not very inspiring. The next worse level is learning environments where you simply click yourself through and get some certificate at the end. Or you have a huge collection of so-called 'learning paths' with more or less well curated content. But nothing really changes here, neither in the company nor with myself. And that's no surprise: Take academic education.

From Monday to Friday, somebody stands before you and teaches about content. Content that the industry is often far ahead of. What we do have is dialog, a face-to-face culture. Learning comes from handling things, the joint solution of problems, from observing and imitating. Still, most companies have learning systems similar to academic ex-cathedra teaching, only in a more modern disguise.

What does the proper development of leaders look like in the digital age?

Let me get back to Allianz, a 130-year-old German insurance company that once worked with a very conservative approach. When I look at #lead and the resulting acceleration platform: It is radical. It's so very non-Allianz-like, and that was the feedback I got. And that made it great because #lead provokes people to rethink leadership. Why? Because the (traditional) way that led us to the present cannot be the way toward future success. It was necessary to shake things up. And I believe #lead has delivered here.

I believe we were more radical, pushed the envelope even farther. I for one don't see what we created as a learning platform. It's an acceleration platform for strategy and transformation. And that's the reason why I like our approach so much. It's what we like doing most: putting together complex content and trying to turn it into something coherent, embedded in an exciting story about the future of our organization.

You have to explain this to me – how can being radical promote leadership culture?

> I for one don't see what we created as a learning platform. It's an acceleration platform for strategy and transformation.

Counterculture promotes culture. Let me give you an example: How does Donald Trump provoked more democracy in the United States by creating counterculture? Because I don't want autocracy. I see what I don't want. At #lead, we worked with personas, introducing a character named 'Dr. No,' i.e. a prototype that says no to everything.

By creating a contrast, a character that counters everything we want to achieve in the leadership culture, we provoke a dialog among our leaders. And that's exciting: Because such a character brings out the core of our leadership culture. Why is that possible? Because we get involved in issues that we may not like. We talked about it earlier: We must avoid only dealing with opinions that correspond to our own. With a character like Dr. No, this discourse is crystallized quite well.

What's special about #lead?

Let's go back to the roots of Allianz: For 130 years, we were organized in a federal structure; each operational unit had its own unique identity; each its own culture, its microculture at Allianz: So if Anna, a team leader in Germany, and Gregg, a team leader in Ireland, were to switch their roles, it would be like going from Mars to Venus, switching from one culture to a completely different culture. We have no common language, no common standard of leadership behavior. With #lead, we have embarked on a shared global dialog to work out what it takes to be a successful leader today.

With the so-called 'leadership passport,' we launched a tool for creating the basis for a uniform standard worldwide. Whether I traveled to Ireland to Sri Lanka, Mexico or Australia, every leader knew the same things and has had the same experience. So we know that the basic knowledge is there. But basic knowledge is not enough: We need to develop solutions that go beyond that and help us build a new leadership culture at Allianz.

So I think the real purpose of our leadership training is to create for all leaders at Allianz a worldwide uniform language and global networks. Just now, we're expanding the platforms for #lead, and the feedback we get is fantastic. For most leaders, the greatest eureka moment is when they're able to speak the Allianz language with people from other countries around the world.

Scotty: The ship's all yours, Sir. All systems are ready and running automatically. A chimpanzee and two interns could fly it!

Captain Kirk: Thank you, Mr. Scott. I won't try to take that personally.

Star Trek

The 11 agile principles of strategy activation

#1 Cadences

The heartbeat of a company, as it were. We've known this for many years. Most corporations report quarterly results, so that key decisions, board meetings, etc., are frequently aligned to the quarterly rhythm. Organizations that apply sprints and iterations also frequently follow this heartbeat. To supplement this three-month rhythm, there is an additional two-week interval for more granular division, the so-called sprints. In some frameworks, these are then bundled in so-called iterations (e.g. every four to five sprints).

Regardless of which setup you choose, the important thing is that the sprints stand for an end date for the completion of work packages (see #2 ➡ 'products' or 'sub-products,' MVP). The new thing about cadences is that they have regularity that is more granular than quarters (some teams even plan for 12 months). And it constantly produces visible results. The so-called 'work in progress,' i.e. permanently not being done and having to wait for one another, is avoided.

When we activate strategies, we usually initiate cadences like these, i.e. teams synchronize with one another every few weeks (e.g. by planning the next iteration) and produce very visible results quickly. This can be made use of for drawing up specific work packages in strategy activation as well as for the team itself that orchestrates the strategy activation (see the example of ➡ Swiss Re: Activation of the global HR function to support the focus on more agility in this playbook).

#2 **Products, subproducts, Minimal Viable Products (MVP)**

The full power of the fast heartbeat unfolds when you agree on delivering finished 'products,' i.e. work packages, after each cadence. This is crucial: The products can be small, 80% 'perfect,' only a subproduct from a larger one – but they have to be finished, visible, tangible. Because this is the only way to ensure that tasks and objectives are not engulfed fully in an opaque melange of 'work in progress,' are obfuscated or even hold up other sub-projects and tasks. A great number of visible results are achieved over a year this way, and you can interfere and direct if they are not the desired results.

The idea of the minimal viable product means to consider right from the onset what actually can be done or made possible in the given time. This is what we then agree on as a 'product.' With each product, you then describe the so-called 'definition of done,' i.e. when do we accept a product as finished. All these considerations happen mainly at the outset. Then you have time for a sprint, an iteration, etc., to deliver.

In strategy activation, we work a lot with products and subproducts because they quickly deliver visible results. You can decide in a timely way whether an activation mechanism works or not; and you can learn directly from it. This brings us to the next principle: managing your own time.

#3 **Managing time, not results**

In traditional project management, you consider how much time and resources you actually need to deliver a certain result. In an agile world, it's the other way round: You think about how much you can actually deliver in the time you have at your disposal. For many people this is a new way of thinking. So if I define my 'product' in an iteration that I want to deliver, I look at my calendar and see I only have 20% of time for it. This means: Instead of promising to deliver, I define the size of my work package such that I will certainly make it in the 20%. Because – and that's the principle of the cadence or the 'product' – the thing I want to deliver must be completed.

#4 Ongoing prioritizing

Companies that successfully activate strategies live one principle quite strongly: Active listening within the organization and the permanent prioritization of their activities. Most of them have commitment surveys and annual surveys among employees, Net Promoter Score (NPS) results, leadership panels, change agents and more, which are excellent sources for finding out where exactly the problems lie (see Chapter ❯ Measure in this playbook).

Using and understanding these sources and deriving from them activities necessary to get the show on the road – therein lies the noble art of strategy activation. Because most companies we have seen come from a world of managing initiatives from start to finish. Permanent prioritization is somewhat the opposite of that: Initiatives are constantly questioned, and only those things are continued that actually yield visible results. And you need to have the courage to terminate anything that does not work.

#5 Retrospectives

In 'The Fifth Discipline,' Peter Senge describes it as the ideal picture of a learning organization: Trying to address the agile world with so-called retrospectives, i.e. the systematic reflection upon the past iterations or sprints and subsequently – here lies the crux of the matter – the immediate application of what has been learned to the next iteration. Because it creates a spiral of learning and getting better as an inherent and permanent part of the process. We use retrospective primarily to establish mechanisms, which constantly question the efficacy of activation steps. Do they accomplish exactly what you want to achieve? If yes, can we scale them globally? If not, why not, and how can we learn from this regarding other activities? By making retrospectives and learning a permanent feature that is directly applied, organizations performing strategy activation can make their activation steps extremely effective.

Such organizations refrained from major change programs designed on the drawing board and pushed through the organization in several waves. Instead, they begin with hypotheses for activities, learn, improve, learn, improve – thus addressing almost to the 'T' the problems or such accelerators that lend full effectiveness to a strategy.

#6 Cross-functional teams

One of the strongest agile mechanisms in strategy activation is building cross-functional teams. The idea has been known from Kaizen for many years: You assemble only those people who, all along the process chain, are vital for the solution of a problem. It's quite similar in an agile world: You look at which problems you want to solve. For this, you don't use functional teams but people who have a sense for problem-solving.

We often use this mechanism to set up teams that manage a strategy activation on their own, i.e. we put together teams from Strategy, Business, HR, Communications, Operations and sometimes even Legal. Frequently, it is nearly a mirror image of the executive management. The advantage is that all topic owners and decision-makers are on one team. Strategy activation cannot be assigned to a specific department such as Strategy, HR or sales. Since strategy activation is targeted at the entire organization, activation steps are highly cross-functional if the team that coordinates them already maps this structure.

#7 Decision-making power on the team

The challenge of cross-functional teams is that in 'conventional' hierarchy, all members of the team need the blessing of the executive in all important decisions – something that makes managing activation steps well-nigh impossible. The agile world provides a principle again: Decisions should be made where they occur. This requires that leaders do actually transfer the much-quoted 'empowerment' to the teams and really give them leeway to make decisions on their own. In companies where this is practiced, powerful results come quickly, while activation steps stand in the way in an environment where policy disputes and decision-making conflicts are the rule.

#8 Transparency & visibility

We use this principle primarily on the teams that coordinate the strategy activations. Whether we apply a simple so-called Kanban Board (i.e. an overview of all activities and work packages) or a systematic tool such as Objectives & Key Results (OKR) – what's crucial is that everybody on the team knows what's happening. This doesn't mean that everybody is involved in everything. On the contrary, the responsibility for work packages should remain with individual or on small teams. By showing everything that is happening at the moment and perhaps even jointly planning, inter-dependencies and connections can be captured quickly and the best use made of the creative power of the group.

#9 The 'customer' as part of the team

Another principle we often see during the implementation of activation steps: Invol-ving those who are directly affected by a 'product.' In our work, especially in major corporations, we often saw how HR and IT departments provide tools and training events that don't reach users at all by going over their heads. From the point of view of the department such offers may make sense, not, however, from the point of view of those working directly in the organization or having immediate customer contact. To avoid this from the outset, some companies deliberately involve the customers (whether internal departments or actual customers out there on the market) directly in the development of a product, service or tool – as a normal member of the team (see the example in ➲ Microsoft: Help shaping a new era – activating Microsoft's strategic core worldwide or Swiss Re: Agile transformation as a movement – when HR activates agility in this playbook). The impact of the support for the actual activation is increased manifold.

#10 Nudging

In recent years, research in behavioral economics has generated exciting insights on how large numbers of people can be motivated to change behaviors radically by simple 'nudges.' The so-called nudge theory and the research done by the behavioral economist Richard Thaler and his colleagues summarize the ideas best. The exciting thing is: Nudges change behavior without prohibiting or imposing anything or offering economic incentives. In its basic features, nudging first defines ideal behavior, the so-called 'default.' The default isn't prescribed to people. Instead, 'nudging' tries to get them to do it themselves by their own behavior. For example: Instead of leaving the boxes empty that are supposed to be checked on a form, they are pre-checked, i.e. the person must de-select them actively.

The result is that the default is more often done than when the check box must be actively marked. Of if paying the invoice from a health insurer takes very long: Studies have shown that a simple sticky note on the invoice saying 'If you transfer the amount within seven days, you help a family of three out of financial difficulties, who must prepay this amount from their own pocket' helps, so that invoices are paid not just after 40 days but in 10 days on average. Nudging has evolved from behavioral economics to marketing. For changing behaviors in organizations, the theory offers great opportunities to transform behavior throughout and without too great an effort.

#11 Digital collaboration

It has certainly been an everyday feature at many global corporations for some time now; for some companies, it only became visible during the COVID-19 pandemic: Working together 'face to face' in one room is not always possible or even wise. Workshop formats, collaborative formats, the presentation of information, learning together or individually – all of this can be done with (sometimes free) digital tools today. In global contexts anyhow, and today also within one company, when working together at the office isn't possible.

This even applies to production employees. Here it is important to provide the infrastructure. Digital collaboration is subject to different dynamics than working out topics together on topics in one room. In his contribution to the five levels of virtual collaboration, Glaveski (cf. Glaveski 2020 'The Five Levels of Remote Work – And Why You're Probably at Level 2') describes how 'copying' the office situation into a virtual setup meets at best the second of a total of five possible maturity levels – because all inefficiencies are also copied without making use of the digital world to get rid of them.

Instead of merely copying, people should adapt to the digital formats of collaboration (e.g. working together in documents, working with collaboration tools). Teams that succeed in working completely asynchronously go one step further. They establish a culture defined by common goals, work principles and results – beyond that, the team members work completely independently (cf. Choudhury 2020 'Our Work-from-Anywhere Future'). According to Glaveski, nirvana is the teams that actually collaborate better without an office. The studies of Choudhury also show that such setups are quite possible.

Why are we describing these levels? Because we want to demonstrate that digital setups have advantages for collaboration if they're used correctly and don't just imitate the office setup. This is true not only for global corporations that are accustomed to this kind of collaboration but also for companies that see themselves suddenly forced to find new ways of collaboration due to a pandemic such as COVID-19; or for companies that want to reduce their CO_2 footprint strategically so collaboration in one room no longer is an option.

Digital mechanisms are technically so mature today that there's no need for compromises in terms of results or activation (see ➤ Acceleration platforms in the Chapter 'Digital tools and platforms for strategy activation.'

How do you know that you're on the right track? **Run things permanently**

When you realize you can rely on your colleagues to activate your strategy, then...

- you won't look any longer for the culprits but seek solutions with your team.

- you'll pat your team's shoulder because this failed attempt has yielded this completely unexpected but ingenious result.

- you'll see decisions no longer in black or white but discern many options.

- you'll look forward to trying out new ideas and make it better instead of waiting for months with it.

- you'll no longer work in silos and isolated solutions with your team but share new findings as early as possible and suddenly realize how much your organization already knows.

- you can hardly wait for the next 'Yes, but...' because such a shared experience will again help to get better.

Measure

The last but quite important chapter on strategy activation is making success visible and, above all, measurable. While measuring the power of the activation is important to show clout and power, it's not easy to establish a direct link to the success of a strategy. Basically, strategy activation can be measured from two perspectives: In relation to activation and in relation to the strategy.

Capture strategy activation in figures

Key figures about the activation steps taken is likely the simplest measure of strategy activation: What is the percentage of employees globally who have worked on something? How many teams have used a new method? How do the results of the South America region compare with those in Asia? Often survey results about activities are on hand or can be easily collected and understood.

> The key to these measurement points is not to confuse them with the success or failure of a strategy.

The key to these measurement points is not to confuse them with the success or failure of a strategy. Because the statements they make relate solely to the activities themselves. We have often seen that Communications departments interpreted the number of people having seen or read a communication as a success of its content – this is, of course, a fallacy. To show that strategy activation is working, you need to answer other questions: How much faster did we put our products on the market? How much customer loyalty were we able to transform into what amount of revenue? How much cost reduction has resulted from higher automation rates in one year – all this with the help of strategy activation? Here measuring is far more difficult because causality is usually not directly understandable and traceable.

When we measure strategy activations in organizations, we look at four dimensions:

1. Identification
Can people identify with the strategy and its goals?

2. Empowerment
Do people feel that they are deployed in such a way that their strengths contribute to the attainment of the strategy?

3. Impact
Do people notice they make a difference through their work with regard to strategy achievement?

4. Collaboration
How do people rate team and departmental collaboration with respect to the collective effort of strategy implementation?

With these four perspectives, we ensure that the basic idea of the activation is achieved, especially when we ask about empowerment and impact. It's not always possible to launch your own questionnaire for the entire organization. This is why many companies make use of the option of ascertaining the success of the activation in existing surveys (with separate questions).

Measure the indirect causality

Nonetheless, we have learned that it's useful to conduct this dialog of indirect causality – especially when historical data are on hand (before the work of strategy activation versus the time afterward). In many cases, at least a comprehensible reference can be made that shows how strategy activation contributes to the attainment of strategic (usually financial) key figures. The article ➜ Microsoft: Help shaping a new era – activating Microsoft's strategic core worldwide, for example, was reviewed as a case study at the London Business School – particularly because a quantifiable connection to the business success could be made.

The advantage of using online activation tools is that they provide a huge multiplicity of data. We also saw in organizations that many data points (up to tracking an improved collaboration) can be collected or are actually already being collected. It's often not done because people don't know that the data exists or can be made usable. Our experience shows that including measurability in the considerations from the onset helps time and again to show the enormous value contribution of strategy activation quantitatively – a 'currency' that is often the only accepted one in the Financial and Strategy departments in companies.

How do you know that you're on the right track? `Measure`

If you measure the right thing in strategy activation, then...

- you will no longer try to 'squeeze' maximum performance out of each individual; instead you ask yourself: With what factors can I measure whether we offer an environment where everybody wants to and is able to make a maximum contribution?

- you will ask: How do I recognize that those who wish to contribute are capable of doing so and are empowered to do it?

- you will search for indicators that show how collaboration is actively practiced on a team level and between areas.

- you'll think about how the personal relation a commitment to (identification with) the shared goals can be improved and how to make the improvement measurable.

- you'll concentrate on the measurability of factors and behaviors that show employees that their dedication and work contribute to the overall success every day, so they experience self-efficacy (impact).

Figure 40: Meaning and significance at work. Excerpt from a Big Picture on the topic of Meaning@Work, TATIN Institute 2023.

STRATEGY ACTIVATION IN MAJOR CORPORATIONS

THOUGHT LEADERS OF A NEW GENERATION

Thought leaders of a new generation

The ideas of strategy activation are applied in companies in the most astonishing ways – the following examples show how strategies can be brought to life throughout a corporation with several thousand employees, who are motivated and feel included. Baloise, Microsoft and Swisscom apply various mechanisms from the Canvas and combine them differently. What they have in common is that they put people, every individual employee, in the center of the activation. The examples are designed to show that activation with several thousand employees is possible, so they will be an inspiration for one's own strategy work.

Baloise Group:
Emotions, people and networks – not processes and hierarchies
By Beat Knechtli

Breaking up existing patterns – the transformation of Baloise Group

The 'Basler Versicherungs-Gesellschaft gegen Feuerschaden' (Basel Insurance Company against Fire Damage) was founded in 1863. Today it is known as the 'Baloise Group' and operates in four countries under the umbrella of Baloise Holding AG. At the peak of its geographical spread in 1938, it was represented in 51 countries worldwide. Baloise can look back on a very eventful history. Despite its history and changing customer needs, there is one principle Baloise has faithfully adhered to throughout time: The principle of safety.

Although financially successful and independent, in 2014 we began with the process of considering the strategic re-alignment of Baloise Group from 2016 onward. With the 'GRIP' strategy phase (Growth and Return Improvement Program, time horizon from 2011 to 2016) through which we were going at the time, the organization pursued a consolidation and process optimization strategy to boost the earning power in the existing business lines and improve attractiveness for investors. As a result, Baloise increased its profitability during this period but shrunk in terms of the number of customers.

Due to the developments in the financial markets and the increasing pressure from new competitors on the market ('fintech startups'), we started as early as in 2014 to try and define the next strategic alignment starting from 2016. Over several iterations, it became obvious that the continuation of the previous strategic alignment with minimal adjustments was out of the question. Differentiation in customer perception was required to be able to grow again.

The shared conviction at the time was that Baloise could only reach this goal through more innovation and the expansion of its previous core business beyond the traditional fields. With the financial independence achieved by the Baloise Group in 2014, we'd earned the right to make a strategic shift to growth, meaning we would enter into greater risk.

The core of the new 'Simply Safe' strategy is a focus on the customer and the customer experience. It's no longer just a matter of covering possible risks and settling them in the event of a loss but of addressing other needs of the customers in a changing societal environment. With a clear focus on the customers and three simple and ambitious goals regarding employees, customers and shareholders, we embarked on a journey toward future growth in 2016. This was a first and meaningful deviation from the tradition of comprehensive number-focused strategy and business plans, which had been the norm in the Baloise up till then.

The three goals at a glance

Employees: Among the top 10% of employers in the sector
Employees are the key to implementing the new strategic alignment. This is why Baloise wants to take a leading position in the industry in terms of employer attractiveness on a European level. The development is measured by a performance indicator that shows how often Baloise is recommended as an employer.

Customers: One million additional customers
Baloise will become the first choice for people who just want to feel safe. With an even more pronounced focus on customer needs, custom-tailored omni-channel communication and innovative products and services in the fields of insurance, assistance and pensions, Baloise will have acquired one million additional customers by 2021. This represents an increase of 30% compared with 2016.

Shareholders/investors: CHF 2 billion cash influx to the Holding
Thanks to the sustainably improved earning power in the life and banking insurance business as well as new innovative products and services, Baloise intends to channel a total of CHF 2 billion in cash to the Holding by 2021. The shareholders profit directly from this because an attractive dividend policy is being consistently pursued and indirectly because targeted investments are made in new strategic projects that generate additional revenue from existing and new business areas.

Developing new patterns – Baloise strategy in the form of a story in six chapters.
If you can offer only a few key figures, you must think about how to make people in the organization listen and participate. A strategy that sounds great on paper and makes sense to top management but doesn't speak to the emotions of customers and everyone in the company, thus making us unique, is nothing but a waste of time and money. Based on this principle, storytelling was the approach that helped us to embark on implementation.

Figure 41:
Strategy story in
six chapters
Baloise Group 2022

Working with the London-based group 'The Storytellers,' we developed a story in 2015 with messages for outside and inside. Stories can be used across cultures and generations; they move people emotionally and help them understand abstract strategies better. They make people contribute stories of their own and make a company unique. Moreover, they are credible and create space for implementation, which is no longer prescribed in micro-management. They have a long service life and are adaptable over time. Last but not least, storytelling is a technique you can learn and pass on.

The dramatic composition of the Baloise 'Simply Safe' story was deliberately designed along an emotional curve with ups and downs. The story forms the basis of the mobilization of all employees, and it was given a persona as the face of the customers: A woman named 'Sarah.' Anything to be considered from a customer's point of view in the future was thus given a reference and was no longer so abstract. Both the choice of a woman as the personification of customers and using a story irritated people and attracted attention.

This curiosity had the desired impact, and the next step could be initiated. The question that now arose was: How do we distribute and embed the story and the strategy in the company?

Identifying existing patterns – social network analysis to mobilize employees

Traditionally, strategies are communicated top-down. They are the pride of top management; in most companies, the strategies are still claimed as an exclusive right of top management to develop and disseminate. At the same time, we know that in many cases a gap exists between top and bottom in the informal structure of organizations and there is little permeability.

Figure 42:
Network analysis,
employees
Baloise Group 2022

After we at Baloise had involved a largish group of employees from various manage-ment levels in a number of iterations as early as during strategy sessions and story development, we were now confronted with the challenge of finding an approach to carry our story and the three very ambitious corporate goals into the hearts and minds of our employees.

As part of my professional experience that stretches across more than 30 years, I had successfully used 'social network analysis' (SNA) at a number of organiza-tions. Social network analysis is a quantitative method for collecting and analyzing relational data. SNA helps us to understand the informal organization. It defines the social network in the company, seen as groups of individuals (teams, departments or organizations) that are linked to one another by relationships (e.g. communication, knowledge transfer, collaboration or trust). In academia, social network analysis has been used successfully for more than 80 years, so it's not exactly new but unknown to many organizations.

SNA helps us to understand the actual organization as a network and identify the nodes in it. The nodes are the influencers who can now work with me to address and handle the question of support and resistance. With the help of a comprehensive employee survey in 2016 on the topics of 'trust' and 'role model,' we identified 250 people out of more than 7,000 employees, who were rated as 'influential' by their colleagues. They came from all levels of the organization; by the way, members of top management are hardly ever among them.

The people identified had to agree in advance that they want to participate. With them and with top management, we then worked through the strategy and story, integrated resistance and criticism and reviewed it all once more. At Baloise, these people are called 'sparks' and they're generally entitled to find their own means and ways of animating their colleagues to engage with strategy and story.

Thus we worked top-down and bottom-up at the same time. This resulted in accelerated dissemination and more open dialogs. Both are desirable and necessary in order to advance the intended transformation. It is completely irrelevant where people come from. Culture and change are far too important to be left to HR and management.

Based on the figures of the employee engagement survey we introduced in 2016 to measure the spread of the strategy along with employer attractiveness, just under 90% of the employees across the Group believed in 2017 that a clear strategic alignment exists and that a discussion with them about the strategy took place. This means we had reached the tipping point with regard to the dissemination and discussion of the strategy. Action was now the order of the day, so ideas were fleshed out in the real world.

Establishing new patterns — playing and experimenting to grow and and challenge more old patterns

Employees of financial service providers in general and of banks and insurance companies in particular are quite averse to risk. There's no doubt that this behavior is a good thing when it comes to the services provided to customers. However, for the strategic realignment of Baloise to disproportional growth and innovation, such behavior is a hindrance. So the next step was about activating the courage to take more risks. Fear of making mistakes and the hope of being successful and becoming visible lie closely together. At Baloise, this motivated us to resort to the power of playing.

People deploy the play element all through their lives. It creates experience, emotions and memories that are imprinted on the mind. We wanted to create such an experience for our employees – an experience that is compatible with the strategy and story of Baloise. In collaboration with and under the aegis of the Communications department of Baloise, 'Sarah's Vision' was created, a collaborative board game. In 2018, i.e. at half-time of the 'Simply Safe' strategy phase, only around one-third of the objectives had been achieved. We intervened with a major group event called 'Impact Event.' The goal was to show employees from all levels where we stood, that we needed to accelerate more to achieve our goals.

Figure 43:
Impact event,
Baloise Group 2022

The Impact Event was organized along five topics that had been identified in advance as bottlenecks for the implementation of the strategy. With around 500 participants from all countries and divided in 21 groups, on this day we hunted for ideas for how we could accelerate implementation and improve results. In total, we came up with 63 ideas, to which we added a 64th idea, namely our board game. Starting from January 2019, we commenced with the implementation.

Figure 44:
Strategy game
'Sarah's Vision,'
Baloise Group 2022

Sarah's Vision is a game that can only be won as a team. It has different game-playing levels. The game-playing situations in the various sections of the organization were accompanied by around 100 moderators, whom we trained specifically for this purpose. After a call on the intranet, they had volunteered in order to make a contribution to the implementation of the strategy.

By mid-2019, we were able to motivate around 4000 employees to employ the play element and learn in order to repeat once more the core strategic messages and invite them to implement them in their personal sphere. With this, we reached more than one-half of all employees of Baloise and were able to build yet another network of 100 strategy ambassadors.

Subsequently, in addition to several prizes for the game and the hashtag '#ourfuture' communication campaign, this approach yielded a visible increase in the growth figures of Baloise, and we were getting closer to our goals defined in 2016. As at October 2020, we already had reached our goal for employees. In the Korn Ferry benchmark, we rank in the top 8% of employers, and 86% of our employees recommend Baloise as employer; response rate: 81%.

We gained more than 635,000 new customers from organic growth. Another 500,000 customers were added through acquisitions. We were able to bring cash amounting to CHF 1.3 billion to the Holding and increase the dividend by around 23%. The total shareholder return is 34% (compared with 21% in the European Insurer Index SIXP benchmark).

Developing patterns – Simply Safe Season 2
Developing what has been learned and continuously providing new stimuli
We were able to achieve or very nearly achieve the goals we had set for ourselves by the end of 2020. It also means: After the game is before the game. Specifically, we've been working since 2019 again to develop the next strategic phase, Simply Safe Season 2 and to roll out the corresponding measures.

In late October 2020, we went public with the Baloise Week. An entire week was dedicated exclusively to the launch of the next strategic phase as of 2022 (until 2025) and the release of the new Story Season 2. During this week, we informed employees and investors of where we stand and what the plans are for the next few years. Due to the circumstances (COVID-19), we had to postpone the occasion scheduled for March 2020 until October 2020 and do it out online, since the legal provisions during the pandemic prohibited an in-person event.

The event attracted a great deal of interest on the part of employees and investors. We were able to reach over 80% of all Baloise Group that week. The response to the Investors' Day was also quite high.

Gert de Winter, Baloise Group CEO, put it as follows: 'I'm very proud of what has been achieved so far. Since the launch of our 'Simply Safe' strategy program, Baloise has met the demands of its most important stakeholders. In addition, Baloise had raised awareness internally of the issues of customer focus, innovation, digital transformation and cultural transformation and set the benchmark within the European insurance industry.'

Figure 45:
CEO at a virtual event,
Baloise Group 2022

With the next strategic phase – Simply Safe Season 2 – Baloise will continue on its successful path and focus even more on the triad of its success: 'employees,' 'customers,' 'investors.' There will be new, ambitious goals in all three dimensions. Alongside the vigorous core business, innovation will play a crucial role in Season 2 in achieving these goals. In tandem with insurance, asset management and banking, innovation initiatives will constitute a mainstay that is expected to contribute to the business and value growth of Baloise with a target value of 1 billion CHF by 2025.

The new goals are:

- **Employees:** To be among the top 5% of employers in Europe – now across all industries

- **Customers:** 1.5 million new customers within four fiscal years – reducing the time necessary, while increasing the target on a new basis of 3 million active customers

- **Investors:** 25% higher cash generation – again CHF 2 billion but in 4 instead of 5 years

So the journey continues with ambitious aims, and we're working on developing new and unusual ways to bolster success. If you'd like to track what's coming, you'll find information at: www.baloise.com and on our Baloise channel on YouTube. There you'll find information on the new strategy Simply Safe Season 2 and videos on Baloise Week, the Investors' Day and the board game Sarah's Vision.

Help shaping a new era – activating Microsoft's strategic core worldwide

By Jean-Philippe Courtois

Microsoft has undertaken one of the most complex transformations in history – reshaping not only its company but also an entire industry. And it is taking a leading role. Strategy Activation was an integral part of this transformation from the very beginning – at global scale. What made this journey so successful (a journey the company is still on)?

The starting point: Fundamentally redefining Microsoft's strategy

Microsoft's transformation is huge: From a technology provider and a business model based on licensing, fees and selling products to a business model based on customer service consumption – and therewith highly interlinked with the success of its very own customers. That meant also to make the most of a massive business opportunity. The migration of computing to the cloud. Yet the strategic challenge is concise: What is the strategic relevance of Microsoft in the new era of 'cloud first, mobile first'? In essence, the answer to this is to build a business service platform. This was back in 2016 and already then, some significant technology shifts started to happen.

So the first years when Satya Nadella joined as our new CEO, he spent a lot of time reengineering all the research and development processes to create a cloud-first organization. From a product development standpoint, this is a huge challenge. You think about 130,000+ employees of which most of them are engineers – a massive change. What we didn't touch yet then, was the front-end, i.e. to move into a customer, service-led business. For becoming a service-led business the question was: How do we embrace that new 'consumption culture'? Historically we have been a company building products, releasing and selling them via licensing (in its most simple terms). Now our culture at Microsoft had to be:

How do we drive our customer's success? So the fundamental shift was from seeing our customers as license buyers every once in a while to helping them deliver their business. This meant as Microsoft we essentially enable digital transformation, which leads to financial success of our customers. That in consequence means we optimize Operations, empower employees, help develop new products and services – and yes also opening up new revenue streams for them. That's huge! Once we have prioritized this as our mantra, it needed a complete redesign of our DNA, our operating mechanisms or our roles, at the end of the day of our organization design – and therewith fundamentally changing the way people work.

It was transforming the way our people operate, redefining the outcomes they drive, redefining the measures of success. For example: Every second of the day we want to make our clients successful in their very own line of business. And that's what we today measure. We can draw a direct connection between customer success and our contribution. In summary: Asking ourselves about our strategic relevance as a company (cloud first, mobile first), providing an answer (service-led business) and then transforming Microsoft to become a leader in this new era.

The foundation: Alignment and strategic capabilities
Building on this redefinition, three areas needed to be managed: A facts and figures-driven business, with the right processes; a global, skilled workforce and technology and from the very beginning doing this together with the customer. How to bring these three elements together?

Part one: Aligning the company on 'solution areas'

First, we decided to align the company on solution areas – i.e. areas of investments, innovations and go-to-market developments. We picked at the time six areas (four in the commercial space, two in the consumer space like gaming and devices). What this means: Instead of having a laundry list of products and services (and we have hundreds and hundreds of them), we only picked six. Which creates immense focus.

And with our management team, which I am part of and meets every Friday, we focus only on where we stand with these six solution areas (e.g. financially, technologically, etc.). One by one.

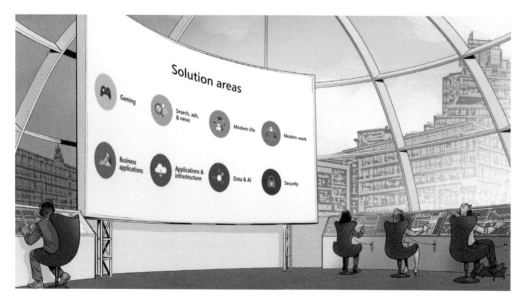

Figure 46:
Defined solution areas in
the transformation program,
Microsoft 2022

Part two: Define few strategic capabilities

Once the company was aligned, we decided to enter the second step of the plan and build the strategic capabilities needed. These eventually translate into personal capabilities. In my own history at Microsoft this was by far the biggest endeavor, as overnight 40,000 people changed jobs. To be precise, what I mean with principles are capabilities needed as an enterprise. And again: Be decisive about them, so for us it was five in essence:

(1) Tech intensity: Develop deeper technical skills in the field, to be able to engage with our customers.

(2) Industry: Investing in deeper industry knowledge as only if we understand the business of our clients we can develop solutions in partnership with them.

(3) Customer success: This is about enabling our customers, i.e. providing them with access to Microsoft innovation as needed, at the speed of us developing them – often with them together.

(4) Shaping our partner ecosystem: We have 340,000 partners globally and we reshaped entirely how we work with them. We built their cloud capabilities with our technology, we helped them sell their own solutions with our technology or we jointly did go-to-markets with them again on our technology.

(5) Digital selling: Clearly, we had to shift our gears, particular for the Small and Medium Size Companies market. And also with remote selling: Combining digital/AI and social selling.

With these five principles we then reshaped the organization, with the functions needed to accomplish the principles. We created one blueprint and instilled it at all subsidiaries across the world. So all type of roles were essentially allocated to a type of organization overnight. We did this deliberately – first gain clarity about what is our strategy, then what are the capabilities needed, then building the organization. Not the other way around (what you often see), which creates a lot of confusion.

Part three: Top management owns the transformation

At Microsoft we operate in two major business organisations: Global Sales Marketing Operations (GSMO), which essentially covers the commercial business in the field across the world (with 14 business units in total and one joint P&L). The other one is Worldwide Commercial Business (WCB), which oversees the global go-to-market strategy as well as services.

This setup comes with two consequences: First both organizations mirror each other – one being in the field, the other providing the capabilities needed. And second: Both leaders of these two organizations define the transformation strategy and own its execution. We partner together very closely: Go-to-market, change management toolset and platform, all the details of (sales) execution to bring into the field.

The three-dimensional activation framework: 'Empower Success'

So far, this all sounds like textbook transformation management. Where did we then instill 'activating' elements, which we think made the transformation so successful to date? And I reflected about this a lot – in the end it is about what change management is all about: What typically happens is you 'reorg' i.e. you tell your people 'this is your new boss, these are your new colleagues, etc....' But this all comes with as little preparedness about the people themselves. And I have seen how the more 'mature' you get, how much time you lose as an organization when you do not align in advance team and people.

So, nine months before the big bang (yes, we went for a big bang), I created a small team. I recruited people who deeply know the business, people from my leadership team, from my commercial business partners...and with transformational leads in every geography in the world. Cross-functional and fully global in nature. With this team we created a framework 'empower success' – meaning empowering your success as an employee. You.

> Everybody thinks of changing the world – but no one thinks of changing himself.
>
> - Leo Tolstoy

You as individual all the way to the leaders and not the other way around. We started with the people, one by one, to make them part of the journey. An exciting journey. And a journey that is tough as we will reinvent the way we will do our sales. Which reminds me of a famous quote: Everybody thinks of changing the world – but no one thinks of changing himself. We addressed transforming at the individual level from the very beginning. The team we then organized around three dimensions or lenses of our activation framework:

'Your growth'

This is all about a fundamentally new learning path of our people. We defined the new roles and with it we created a learning path, in order to learn and digest a lot more knowledge on (1) technology, (2) industry and (3) coaching skills. These three are the three legs of our people development.

Figure 47:
Prioritizing in the
transformation program,
Microsoft 2022

To create impact, we put in place a very exhaustive learning platform – which today is not only used by us but also by our customers – providing a magnitude of content. And people need to get certified (depending on their role) i.e. they need to meet a certain level of proficiency. Plus, leaders must connect and discuss with their team members one-on-one what their take-aways are, what they could have done better and what is their individual learning plan for the next four months to come. So there was an ongoing development discussion to be skilled and trained on the new job.

Now this part is tricky of course – as you ask for personal development and concurrently you don't want to portray an image of 'your current skills and capabilities do not fit our strategy anymore.' A narrative you unfortunately find in many capability development projects or change programs – if not explicitly, then for sure implicitly.

Hence for us we deliberately built on both: The capabilities people bring into Microsoft, founding on their existing professional experience. And then pair it with the capabilities yet to be learned. While the first provide trust and acknowledgment, the latter provide outlook and opportunity. Both, existing and complementary skills, eventually made our capability framework.

At Microsoft we follow the idea of positive leadership – i.e. building on the passion of our people. That makes a big difference: We all have areas of developments, for sure. But when you think about why people join a job, they do this for a purpose, for a meaning. If you don't feel the passion or clearly address the way people can contribute, then you miss a huge opportunity. Hence you must build on the existing capabilities and passions of people.

'Your Success'

We looked a lot at our tooling, particularly digital tools, to embed the new consumption culture. This lens is to manage the business through tools like a customer relationship management (CRM), with artificial intelligence (AI), in short: To be best guided and supported as individual. And, of course, to equip people with content and knowledge of the tools.

'Agility'

This lens is on how we orchestrate all the resources and roles we have globally as a company, in order to enable our customer's success. To make the collaboration as flawless as possible. As simple as it sounds – this still for us is a learning journey we are on. We put the individual at the center of our transformation – and we instilled a couple of activating mechanisms along the way. Let me bring this down to a few activating mechanisms which had the greatest impact to us.

Big bang approach

At Microsoft we wanted to be most impactful as a tech company, so we decided to go for a big bang rather than a soft launch. This does not mean that the transformation itself may take many years, yet for us something else was crucial: Our customers haven't transformed into digital companies yet. So at the end of the day we simply needed to be faster so that we can be a leader in digital transformation. The activating element of this approach was the strong alignment across leaders and teams.

And you need trust – this is the key factor. Because who do you trust in a company? Your team. At Microsoft we essentially started with a very small alliance and created this trust. So we created trusted relationships early on. Then we went broader, again to create trust and alignment. In the end there was a trust spill-over from team to

team, and you experienced that at Microsoft you can rely on authentic leaders.
Provide the why and sense of urgency – leave the how and what open.
What big bang didn't mean for us was to have the architecture outlined in full detail. Yes, we had a pretty solid plan. Not perfect, but we had a plan. And this plan we filled by our people. So we shared the plan early on to gain solidity and again alignment.

This happened through in-depth workshops and discussions, from which we again learned a lot and made it part of the plan. During the activation we put a lot of effort into providing a solid understanding of why we needed to change – and then make everybody see that in fact we need to change. Yet then we halted and actively invited to have intense discussions on how to change and what are we going to do differently.

And this is a powerful moment as this typically is done by selected chosen leaders or sometimes even external consultants. Yet we invited our very own people to define the change. As we don't only need support from them on this journey, in fact we wanted their very input! This we did for months: Providing the why and the sense of urgency, the how then came from our people themselves.

Providing context and tools. Learn. Repeat

At Microsoft we literally created a learning organization: Every week, every month we checked what was not working – and then made it work. Through in-depth workshops and discussions, we were able to provide context and the tools needed. Through very close feedback loops we then made sure that we reflect and learn and adapt the context and tool provision accordingly. In essence, employees at Microsoft defined the change measures and leaders made sure that they can be implemented as smoothly as possible.

Global aspiration with regional characteristics

Our mission as a company is global. And, of course, markets are regional. Hence the regional CEOs were the owners of bringing the commercial strategy to life – and hence also its activation. In fact, every employee at Microsoft interprets the mission personally and within a country or region. Similar to what I shared earlier above: We provide empowerment at management level to facilitate 'local fabrics.'

Refreshed leadership principles

We finally created a number of new key leadership principles – together with all 20,000 managers across the globe: 'Model, coach & care' is our new framework, which clearly underpins the activation spirit we have embarked on. What this means in concrete terms is that as leader you adhere to...

Clarity –
i.e. any one of us needs to bring clarity in everything we do.

Energy –
i.e. be intentional with teams, customers and elaborate on what are the positive vibes. This includes the sometimes tough feedback we share.

Success –
i.e. how do we enable our people to be successful and therewith our customers to be successful.

We brought these principles to our entire leadership community – and decided together to model, coach and care around these three principles.

Positive leadership and consistency:
Lessons learned from 40,000 people transforming

If I look back – and we are not ready yet – I would see a couple of take-aways from what we have learned so far. Clearly, we should have insisted more on digital tooling for our people and instilled more direct feedback loops across teams. The latter is so important that you systematically share knowledge and experiences and build on them (rather than having them sit in a meeting).

Yet for us, we had two strong accelerators on our journey: On the one hand at Microsoft we had an obsession of teaching and educating people about the change. All the time (see Chapter ➲ 'Providing context' Learn. Repeat earlier). And this is far more than just communication: It is about showing, role-modeling, all the time! On the other hand, empowering our people to find the solutions themselves (instead of telling them what to do), that created immense momentum. And as leaders we show that this is our approach and we really mean it.

Where do we stand today from where we started? We are at the dawn – and we made good progress we can be proud of. Financial outcomes are what people see and those results are solid. The journey ahead of is to gain even deeper industry knowledge – which we do together with key industry players. And then there is of course ambitions like scaling our business and embracing certain sectors. But the approach we have taken: To put the individual at the center of our transformation, support them as best as we can and to invite them to own the problem-solving: That is something unique, and we at Microsoft are proud of it.

Playful, interactive and fun: 'Come and join' at Swisscom

By Oliver Stein & Adrian Bucherer

Starting point

Embedding and implementing a strategy is one of the most important tasks of top management. It requires leadership skills, perseverance and discipline in huge amounts. The hearts of employees must be reached and the next major milestone as well as the way to it need to be explained, so that employees are dedicated to and motivated for their work. Fleshed out with powerful pictures and well-formulated sentences, new strategies are often communicated in animated PowerPoint presentations to employees via the various management levels. With give-aways or screen-savers and posters throughout the company, the new visual and content language is made visible; leaders present the new strategy to their teams.

And yet, after a few months, many companies find that employees haven't internalized the new terms as quickly as they would have liked, despite all the effort. Because a personal and substantive examination of the strategy is missing. It's not enough to re-rail campaigns and communicate them. Employees need to grapple with them personally.

In 2018, Swisscom's management succeeded in summarizing the vision, values, the promise, the strategy, the goals and the transformation on one single slide under the heading 'Swisscom Story.' The Swisscom Story was a good starting point, but the real challenge was to develop new and effective ideas to nail down the strategy. That's precisely what we took on with such a marathon task in the private customer division at Swisscom. We wanted to rethink embedding strategy and use new approaches to augment existing, successful formats such as the roadshow, internal TV or executive training in a meaningful way. Because the mood in the private customer division was depressed owing to several restructuring measures, declining customer satisfaction and an unusually high number of disruptions in the network. The management of the private customer division mandated us with picking an approach that would link employees to the new Swisscom Story and rekindle their inner fire for Swisscom.

And this in a decentralized organization across Switzerland with almost 100 Swisscom shops, 10 call center sites and more than 10 different work locations with almost 6,000 employees. The specific aim: To fill the Swisscom Story with life in the SAS (Sales and Services) organizational unit, which is primarily geared toward customers. In other words, the design challenge was: How do we convey the Swisscom Story so that employees can connect to it with both heart and mind and live it with enthusiasm and pride in their day-to-day work?

Approach: Hear, Create, Deliver

For the implementation of our design challenge, we have chosen the 'Hear, Create, Deliver' method. This human-centered design method has been used by Swisscom for more than 10 years in product and process management. Its origins lie in IDEO, an innovation agency in Silicon Valley. It begins with the 'Hear' phase: An in-depth understanding of users and customers – employees, in this case. Followed by 'Create,' the creative phase, where ideas and approaches are discussed. In the third phase of 'Deliver,' initial prototyping, testing and implementing based on iterative principles is aimed at.

Hear

In numerous interviews at all levels of the company, it became clear that front-line workers had little or no use for management terms such as 'lean management' or 'agility.' Topics concerning customers that had to be dealt with on a daily basis, e.g. 'customer orientation,' were repeated often. Enthusiasm for their work at the customer interface was clearly palpable.

When we asked employees how they apply the vision or practice the values in day-to-day work, it became clear that most of them were thinking about these things for the first time. Though they had heard and understood individual terms in the very short team meetings, they weren't able to translate them to their day-to-day work. For them it was clear what simplicity means for the solution of customer concerns, for instance, but they were unable to establish any connection to the Swisscom strategy. We realized we needed to create a platform where employees were empowered to fill the Swisscom story with their own ideas and notions, thus being able to connect it to topics like simplicity or agility in their day-to-day work. It absolutely could not be about reciting the beautifully worded sentence from the mission statement; people needed to bring the values to life with their own stories and their own experience and understand them.

Was management ready to give them this freedom and support the process of nailing down the strategy? Would managers appear in front of employees as facilitators so as to trigger energy and enthusiasm and talk to employees on an equal basis about their experience?

Create

We started the Create phase with an ideas workshop and many participants who think openly and creatively. More than 50 ideas evolved. Every idea was expounded visually on a DIN A4 sheet and then pre-prioritized by a small team. There were hardly any completely new approaches, since we had already tried out a great many formats at Swisscom, given that it is an ICT company.

All ideas selected had to be based on the following design principles:

- promoting the employees' understanding of the customer journey as well as the dialog with management;

- the focus is on the vision and values;

- the handling of the topic should be done by the employees in their everyday work; and

- no PowerPoint presentations or posters are to be used.

The three best ideas were visualized in more detail, provided with initial prototypes and presented to top management for selection.

Figure 48: The top 3 ideas are visualized to present them to management, Swisscom 2022

'You write the Swisscom Story' (center in the picture) clearly won, and the idea that all employees help write the story had full support from top management. We immediately started to create initial prototypes. The basic idea was a booklet that was intended to motivate employees to write their own Swisscom Story. Gamification elements were to be connected with audacious examples.

It was also important to us that the book strengthened the dialog between supervisors and management. It was a 'coloring book': write, rip out and share with others. Using QR codes, the personally filled-out pages could be uploaded on a cloud-based Swisscom solution for all employees.

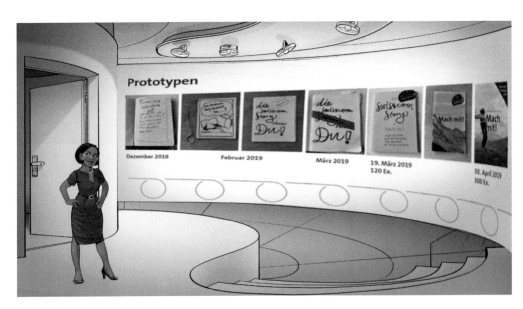

Figure 49: Development of prototypes over time, Swisscom 2022

The ideas became visible and could be compared to other ones. In addition, posts on Instagram could be tagged with the #swisscomstory hashtag. As part of the development of the prototypes, the title morphed from 'You write the Swisscom Story' into 'Come and join.' After just a few weeks, we were able to present the prototypes to middle management and collect their feedback.

The first response was often to say that our creative 'join in' approach was too 'child-ish' and playful for employees. Thanks to the interactive prototype workshops, we were able to take on this objection, test it and refute it. When filling out the forms, critics realized that even simple tasks posed great challenges. And that handling issues in a playful way can be lots of fun.

Deliver
Enriched by the feedback from the prototype workshops and a leadership dialog with the 70 top technical and management leaders, we began the production of the next prototype version following the principle of Iterate and Learn. 'The booklet alone is not sufficient,' was the conviction gained from the workshops. We wanted to engage management in a full-scale dialog with the employees. So we developed the idea of 'Story Cafés,' where the personal stories of the various values took center stage.

But in what sort of dimension should the whole thing take place? With all 6,000 employees, with 3,000 or only a 1,000? When the booklets were released, we agreed with management to test the 'Story Cafés' at three sites and to engage in a closely-focused dialog with the Switzerland-wide roadshow toward the end of the year.

At the same time, we developed a concept for how to distribute and communicate the booklets within the organization. In major organizational units such as the call center, the shops and with locally organized service technicians, dissemination and introduction by team leaders had to be ensured. We included a small guide for the story booklets (like a package insert for medicine), so that employees could begin with their version of the Swisscom Story without a lot of introductory rigamarole. So we made it possible that the booklets were sent directly from the printers to the shops and the major call center sites.

Conclusion

The new participatory approach was met with great enthusiasm and interest among employees. Many immediately drew their version of the digitization monster and posted it on Instagram via the hashtag #swisscomstory. Many used the playful and informative elements for joining in, built paper gliders or tested the 'ring-the-bell.' Several hundred uploads to the cloud server were a testimony to the great interest on the part of employees. In employee surveys, we were also able to identify a significant effect on the transformation levers. Employees now knew the topics better and passed them on.

One year after the introduction and without further communication measures, we were still getting booklet orders at the end of 2020. We had to reprint twice, and the booklet also met with great interest in other Swisscom divisions, although the examples given were heavily geared to the challenges in the private customer segment. Our shop managers were thrilled. Some reported that they simply present Swisscom to new employees by handing them the 'Join In!' booklet.

During the great roadshow at the end of the year, the Join-In book was integrated in the pitches of the management, and the best Join-In pictures were shown. The dialog platforms were smaller than originally planned, less intense and less orchestrated.

Figure 50: 'Ring-the-bell' as an unusual measure for employee activation, Swisscom 2022

The cross-divisional collaboration was particularly positive: Business units developed this approach hand in hand with HR, Experience Designer and top management and shared the responsibility for implementation.

Although the Join-In idea was not implemented as consistently as we would have liked, we saw that strategy activation works with playful and interactive elements and has an impact on a broad basis in a short time. The fact that our Join-In booklets are still ordered by employees – the actual target group of our design challenge – more than 18 months after the launch definitely shows that this approach can be a great augmentation to traditional methods of embedding the strategy. Or have you ever heard of companies where employees in the field voluntarily ask for the printed form of the mission statement and use it as an introductory tool for new colleagues? From our point of view: Mission complete!

Agile transformation as a movement – when HR activates agility

By Ulrich Tennie

Background: Technology-related changes in the insurance industry

The Swiss Re Group is a leading global reinsurer, direct insurer and provider of insurance services. The mission of Swiss Re: 'We make the world more resilient.' With their headquarters in Zurich, Switzerland, where Swiss Re was founded in 1863, it employs around 15,000 people in 80 offices and 23 countries worldwide.

The Swiss Re Group is divided into three divisions: reinsurance (Re), direct insurance for companies (Corporate Solutions) and digital B2B2C insurance (iptiQ). Each division provides solutions to specific customer groups: From major insurance companies to global corporations to larger SMEs. Like other traditional industries (such as media, retail trade, banks), the insurance industry has undergone significant technology-related changes in recent years.

Fundamental technical changes (automation, data analytics, digital sales) and changing customer expectations (especially in terms of better connectivity, customer experience and improved efficiency) confronted insurance companies with the challenge of having to change fundamentally. In this context, Swiss Re sallied forth to implement internal improvements, e.g. to use existing data better and digitize or automate core work processes; as well as to initiate activities geared toward the outside, e.g. the development of new digital products and the expansion of business models through new partnerships.

To translate such strategic initiatives into reality, the management of Swiss Re felt that a fundamental transformation within the company was necessary. From the perspective of top management, the organization had to become far more 'agile' and 'more mobile, faster, more courageous and connected.' Only this way would it be possible to identify new opportunities, address new customer requirements and offer innovative solutions in order to survive in a changing environment.

In the second half of 2018, the development toward more organizational agility, which was already partially underway, was given the decisive impetus and from now on had top priority. On the question of how the planned change ought to be implemented, the Swiss Re leadership deliberately opted against a major transformation 'in one fell swoop.' By contrast, the opinion predominated that it would not fit with their corporate culture and would be counterproductive to introduce agility in a top-down manner. Agility should spread and develop as a kind of movement from bottom to top ('grass roots') and thus grow organically.

This kind of approach seems to be exactly what McKinsey in a 2019 study on successful agile transformations calls the 'emergent' (self-developing) archetype. In this approach, the individual business units have a great deal of freedom for how they want to implement the transformation. The leaders only specify their expectations and set the direction. The other two archetypes in the McKinsey study are 'All-In' and 'Step-by-Step'; in both cases, the approach is much more defined as top-down, including binding changes in the organizational structure.

For Swiss Re, as at September 2018, management clearly expressed the expectation that the organization 'needs to become a lot more agile within the next two years.' All executives were encouraged to strive for more agility in their own areas. How this goal was to achieved in detail was deliberately left open. In early 2019, a whole array of transformation efforts were underway: From small changes, e.g. the introduction of agile methods at team level, up to complex changes of the operating model in two IT units with around 500 employees. So while there were numerous different attempts that developed organically, there was at all times clarity about the direction for the company as a whole. Despite the diversity of leadership-culture initiatives, the same approach should be applied throughout the enterprise.

This common approach was expected to be decisive for development toward greater agility. A rather conservative and hierarchical style of leadership was to be transformed into a courageous, 'purpose-driven' one, enabling each employee to perform leadership tasks on their own ('leadership from every seat'). The leadership culture they wanted was expressed in the definition of desired behaviors: 'Be courageous, adapt at speed and create a joint movement.'

Figure 51: 'Leadership from every seat' as a guiding principle for the new leadership culture, Swiss Re 2022

The dual challenge for Human Resources (HR): agile for the company and agile for HR

The challenge for the HR function was twofold: The department had to decide how it would support the development toward more agility, especially the desired change in leadership culture ('agile for the company'). And secondly, it had to find out how to become more agile itself ('agile for the HR function').

If Swiss Re had opted for a top-down transformation, the answer to the first question would have been quite simple. The contribution of the HR function would probably have been bundled and directed in a work group as part of the overall transformation. But they had deliberately decided against such a top-down transformation. The task was therefore not to support a well-thought-out and structured transformation but to become a part of a movement that quickly picked up pace and consisted of many mini-transformations.

Faced with this situation, HR managers made the decision to rethink HR's contribution and reorganize the department: A small group of volunteers, who all wanted to learn about agility and experiment with new ways of working, was mandated to find out how HR could best support the new agile movement. The answer: By organizing itself in an agile model.

Thus the agile path for HR started with no more than eight people in a room, including the author of this article, several colleagues from a global center of expertise and two global HR partners. We called ourselves the 'People Circle' to express the fact we wanted to work as a cross-divisional team and not be bound by the existing organizational structure.

From the outset, we put a big focus on using tools that are usually applied to agile working. This way, we'd learn from practice on a first-hand basis. To develop a common vision, we began with a so-called V2MOM session (**V**ision, **V**alues, **M**ethods, **O**bstacles, **M**easures). The purpose of such a V2MOM is to clarify the direction and focus the team's energy on the desired outcome. We wanted to concentrate on something that would make a difference throughout the organization, not only in the HR function. So we formulated for ourselves the vision 'to impact and co-determine the agile transformation of Swiss Re and foster change in corporate culture.'

Our contribution was primarily to aim at bringing about change in the Swiss Re leadership culture. We felt that the HR function could have a significant influence on agile transformation at an early stage and make its own important contribution. We were inspired here by experts from the Agile World such as Pete Behrens (see Chapter ➲ Bibliography).

According to these experts, the shift to greater agility is successful if it takes place from inside out and brings about a change in attitudes about value as well as the leadership style (i.e. corporate culture). According to this theory, employees reject change if it initially deals with organizational structure, e.g. the reorganization of the reporting lines (from outside toward inside).

Swiss Re drives forward the topic of agility as a 'movement.' The HR function supports change from the inside out, starting with the corporate culture.

Figure 52: Change beginning with the corporate culture, Swiss Re 2022

After establishing the People Circle, we tackled the challenges facing the HR function in two ways: For one, we decided to focus on the change of leadership culture ('leadership from every seat' and 'agile for the company'). In actual practice it means we must find a way to ensure that managers and teams on all levels (virtually all the 15,000 employees) would begin to adapt their behavior and act more agile, become more courageous, adjust their attitudes quickly and drive things forward in their sphere of influence.

Secondly, we initiated the development toward more agility for the HR function ('agile for the HR function') by starting to work with agile methods, as described below, in the People Circle itself.

How we understand our task as 'activation' and position ourselves as an agile team

The next step involved how to support change best in the leadership behavior within the organization. Right from the start, we found that we should take a look at our role as an 'activation' of the desired leadership culture.

Accordingly, we asked ourselves what we had to do for the new behaviors to pre-dominate on all levels throughout the organization: To be discussed, practiced and finally accepted by many. With this activation approach we explicitly opted against what HR functions of companies often do: Namely to question and adapt their own processes, e.g.: How should we change our compensation policy or our talent management to support the agile movement? We were of the opinion that such efforts were important and needed to be made at a later stage.

Right now, they would not contribute to spreading and exemplifying new behaviors. In addition, it would take far too long to be effective.

Hence we focused on the 'activation' of the entire organization (all 15,000 employees), in particular on three levers or three groups of people:

1. Activating leaders: Enshrining agile leadership ('leadership from every seat')

2. Activating teams: Promoting a dialog on agile behavior in the context of the individual teams; gain a common understanding of existing deficits

3. Activating HR partners: Advanced training for HR partners worldwide so they support their business with the implementation of agile behavior and corresponding ways of working

> With this goal in mind, we wanted to 'activate' ourselves as a team of HR practitioners.

With this goal in mind, we wanted to 'activate' ourselves as a team of HR practitioners. With the help of an agile coach, we turned the People Circle into an agile team, using a number of agile practices on purpose: In order to set up the overall team structure, to establish the coordination mechanisms among the three teams; and to define the processes in the individual teams.

Of the ten practices of agile teams that Stephen Denning describes in his classic textbook 'The Age of Agile' (2018), nine were ultimately applied: working in small groups; small, cross-functional teams; clearly defined work packages; autonomous teams; consistent attainment of goals ('getting to done'); daily stand-up meetings;

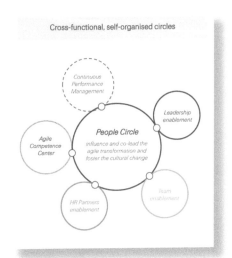

Cross-functional, self-organised circles

Continuous
Performance
Management

Leadership
enablement

Agile
Competence
Center

People Circle

*Influence and co-lead the
agile transformation and
foster the cultural change*

HR Partners
enablement

Team
enablement

Figure 53a:
Target group focus
in the activation of
the HR function,
Swiss Re 2022

radical transparency; customer feedback for every incident; retrospective evaluation and learning. The only method from Denning's list we couldn't implement was: 'Work without interruption,' because our team members only spent a limited portion of their working hours (15-25%) on the People Circle; of course, ideally they would be 100% available to the team in terms of their time.

Overall set-up in the form of three teams that belong together

Agile practices: *small, cross-functional teams, autonomous teams*
We created three teams for the areas of leaders, teams and HR partners, which organized themselves; and called each of them a circle. Each circle had six to eight members, including a product owner and a scrum master. The product owners were responsible for the overall management and in particular for ensuring that the (internal) customers got what they wanted. The scrum masters organized the path there. The six colleagues who assumed these roles were trained in the required techniques 'Just In Time'; for this purpose, they attended external courses (for example with Scrum Alliance, Adventures with Agile).

We made an effort to have members from various areas in each circle so that all skills needed to arrive at an innovative and custom-tailored solution were represented on the team. The 'Leadership Circle,' for instance, included the Head of Executive Leadership Development, who was the product owner, as well as experienced managers from different divisions and regions.

Regular coordination and voting among the circles

Agile practices: *limited ongoing work; consistent goal attainment*

We decided to work toward so-called Minimal Viable Products (MVPs) to be achieved inside of six months ('Getting to Done'). It was therefore vital to arrive at a result within this time-frame. In this way, we would be able to contribute to the developing movement and even accelerate it.

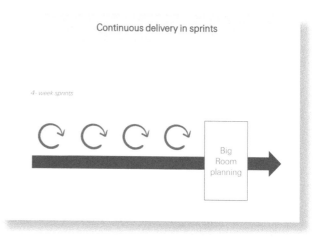

Continuous delivery in sprints

4- week sprints

Big Room planning

If things took a bit longer than six months, it meant we missed the opportunity of helping to shape the movement. We established regular four-week work cycles and a sequence of larger meetings with 25 to 35 attendees, in which the entire People Circle met with internal and external guests. This consistent rhythm was applied to all three circles and meant that we showed one another how far we'd come, asked for internal feedback and discussed the next steps.

Figure 53b:

Applying agile methods: work rhythm in sprints, Swiss Re 2022

Tightly-focused, flexible work processes within one circle

Agile practices: *working in manageable amounts; radical transparency; daily stand-up meetings; customer feedback with every incident; retrospective evaluation*

Each of the three circles worked with agile methods at their own discretion. The circle handling HR partners, for example, divided the development of a two-day Experience Lab into 13 individual program modules such that they could be handled by 13 teams, each consisting of 2 to 3 people, at the same time.

This enabled us to split the challenging task of developing an interactive event involving a broad range of competencies, departments and speakers into manageable units that could be tackled without having to be an expert in the development of workshops. We recorded day-to-day progress on a table (Kanban board) that was accessible to everyone. Thus we were able to make course corrections and send team members where they were needed most.

As part of the first Experience Lab in Zurich, we scheduled a substantially longer session for customer feedback, in which the members of the workshop brainstormed together with us on what should be improved. This brainstorming in turn served as input to our retrospective evaluation, where we discussed what we'd learned and what needed to be changed in version two. The evaluation took a journey around the world, to New York, Hong Kong, Bratislava and finally back to Zurich.

Activating the entire organization with new leadership policies, pulse surveys of teams and worldwide Experience Labs for HR partners

Each of the three self-organizing circles (leaders, teams, HR partners) was geared to developing an activation mechanism that introduced the desired leadership behaviors (be courageous, adapt at speed, create a joint movement) and allowed for active commitment in the relevant group.

Activation focused on 3 key groups – all leaders, all teams, all HR partners with clear deliverables within 6 months

Leaders

Teams

HR Partners

	Leaders	Teams	HR Partners
Activation Mechanism	• Embed new target leadership behaviors for **all 15000 employees** (Leadership-from-Every-Seat)	• Facilitate dialogue to drive more agility within **all 1000 teams**	• Experience Labs to upskill all **100 HR Partners** globally and start addressing actual team challenges
Minimum Viable Products (within 6 months)	• Definition and roll-out of new leadership imperatives that are applicable to all employees • Integration as "HOW" element of performance discussion	• Implementation of first employee pulse survey on Agility that measures the progress on the adoption of the new leadership behaviours (repeated in 6-month cycles) • Toolkit for how to run a pulse results session with a team	• Roll-out of 2-day Experience Labs in 5 locations bringing together HR Partners and Managing Directors, solving actual business challenges • Activation tool kit for HR Partners
Further deliverables (after 6 months from launch, driven by different circles and teams)	• Roll-out of continuous performance management (rating-less) • 2-day leadership development program for all Managing Directors ("Shaping culture for agility & change") • Pathfinder experience for 100 senior leaders with track record of successful change	• Feedback App allowing for giving and receiving immediate feedback • Peer recognition program Cheer4You in selected agile teams	• Follow up work to embed full agile organisational set ups in several teams following Experience Labs • HR Learnfest(s) in all locations around the world for all 420 HR staff to introduce topic of agility

 Swiss Re

Figure 53c: Target group focus in the activation of the HR function, Swiss Re 2022

New leadership policies were drawn up and implemented for the leaders. To live up to the concept of **leadership** on all levels, we took a step that was logical but pretty radical for Swiss: To develop only one version of the leadership policies for all 15,000 employees. Up till then, there were special policies for leaders with HR responsibility and a second version for all other employees.

These leadership policies should be as clear as possible on the question of the type of behaviors employees ought to employ in accordance along the line of 'be courageous, adapt at speed and create a joint movement.'

> Then we introduced the new policies in a number of meetings and video conferencing worldwide.

Then we introduced the new policies in a series of meetings and video conferences worldwide. To achieve a lasting impact, we integrated the new leadership policies, more precisely: The definition of the target behavior, in the HOW dimension of performance management. With this, the behavior would be addressed in regular feedback discussions and at the end of the year; it would be relevant to the bonus; it would likely be perceived as important; and it would find a place in the everyday language of employees and supervisors.

For the **teams,** we introduced a dialog format that would result in a team conversation on the aimed-for agile behavior. We used the existing platform of the annual employee survey for this, transforming it into an 'agility pulse survey.' We defined various questions to measure to what extent the desired behavior was shown; in this way, each team received its own agility index. To activate all 1,000 or so teams, we provided a toolkit that enabled every team to hold a 2-hour agility pulse meeting. The teams were thus able to discuss their own results and draw up measures in an action plan that would make the team more agile. Since mid-2018, we have done the agility pulse surveys every six months. The teams are thus repeatedly given the opportunity to assess their success and make adjustments. For the **HR partners,** we developed an highly-focused interactive two-day event we called 'Experience Lab' that was attended by 20 to 25 HR partners.

Figure 53d: Based on the Kincentric Index, Swiss Re 2022

We held this workshop at five locations worldwide so we reached all 100 HR partners. The goal was to turn the HR partners into expert contact persons for leaders and their teams to discuss the subject of agility. The workshop consisted of a mix of teaching and interactive modules on content that is especially relevant to the HR partners: Agile leadership, organizational design and agile HR practices.

A module on the afternoon of the second day, when the HR partners were paired up with senior managers, turned out to be especially effective. Each of the leaders was asked to bring with them a real example from their business and present it to the group. Then the case was worked on by the participants in groups of five, applying the agile techniques acquired in the workshop. This way, across all locations, around 20 case studies with completely different problems were worked on, e.g.: Accelerate the development of customer solutions for a specific global customer segment; boost efficiency in the processing of insurance claims in a regional service center; re-alignment of a global function in the finance area on account of new regulatory requirements.

> Each of the leaders was asked to bring with them a real example from their business and present it to the group.

Through the work of the People Circle, we activated three groups (leaders, teams, HR partners) and we reached virtually all 15,000 employees. Not only was the collective addressed by general communication – each individual in his or her personal work environment became familiar with the ideas through team dialog meetings and discussions with supervisors.

After the initial activation phase – which was completed within six months – we dissolved the People Circle as planned, and the operational work was taken over by the respective experts and the global HR partners. Just how successful the chosen approach to activation actually was could be gleaned from the fact that a team of no more than eight people in a very short period of time succeeded in achieving tangible progress with 15,000 employees on a non-trivial issue, such as the development of a new leadership culture.

Our most important findings from this work

We in the People Circle have learned something in two ways: one, in terms of the activation of an organization toward a new leadership culture; and second, in terms of our own experience with the application of agile practices.

First insight: Choosing the 'activation' approach is effective for initiating the kick-off of the transformation on a broad basis; after this, further action is needed

The 'activation' approach – unlike a campaign (see the distinction between the two concepts in this playbook) – was sensible and successful from our point of view. In stark contrast to triggering a hierarchical cascade of meetings, one level at a time, addressing many employees as quickly as possible – in our case, the three groups of leaders, teams and HR partners – worked quite well (see other ➜ Activation mechanisms described in this playbook).

In our opinion, this was the right way to raise awareness on the part of a majority of employees for a change that was necessary and actually to achieve initial behavioral changes. Our experience confirmed our presumption: If you want to impact a major emergent company-wide movement, you have to act quickly and aim for maximum reach. Several of the activation mechanisms used have proven to be very effective: Integrating the desired behavior in performance management; ensuring team-level dialog (allowing teams to understand in their immediate context what was expected of them and to determine their own contribution); HR partners and leaders developing specific action plans together as part of the Experience Labs.

Our regular agility pulse surveys allowed us to measure progress and help keep leaders and their teams 'on their toes.' Leaders who were initially skeptical had to realize that agility is no short-lived fad that can be easily sat out. Every six months, they were asked to discuss with their team progress regarding the five specific agile behaviors. A crucial factor of success was defining unambiguously what is expected of leadership behavior and integrating these expectations in performance management.

> Our regular agility pulse surveys allowed us to measure progress.

But to overcome deeply rooted behavioral patterns and achieve a lasting change in leadership behavior (leadership on all levels), more action was needed. To this end, a number of precise leadership development interventions were developed and implemented under the direction of the Head of Executive Leadership Development (see Chapter ➲ Bibliography under Schlüter).

Second insight: setting up an agile team to solve an urgent complex problem (in our case: How can be initiate change in the leadership culture?) is an excellent opportunity to get agile transformation in the HR function off the ground.

We in the People Circle were pioneers who led the movement and at the same time learned a great deal about agility ourselves. We learned, for instance, that learning by doing is the right way to get to the heart of the agility idea. We agree with Darrell Rigby et al. (2020), who noted: 'At the heart of the agile approach is the agile team. If you don't understand how an agile team works, you'll have trouble transferring the agile way of working to the whole company.'

For ambitious HR practitioners and change managers, this means they can only be credible when it comes to higher-level topics such as agile leadership and agile organization if they have experience in agile practices from their own daily work. For example, it was quite helpful to apply all the above methods when working in the People Circle. We found that most of us already knew and used these methods. But the simultaneous and conscious application of all methods created a common language, and the experience was all the more effective.

As a result, we can say: Achieving what we accomplished would have been extremely difficult if we had proceeded the usual way, with everybody on their own in their own field; if we hadn't brought together so many different colleagues from a wide range of divisions in the People Circle to proceed as an agile team with a more comprehensive, common vision. Based on great experience in the People Circle, the HR function of Swiss Re today sets up agile teams as standard practice; especially when it comes to complex, cross-divisional challenges (see the ➲ Bibliography under Snowden). In addition, nearly all HR teams have adopted some of the agile methods, e.g. working in sprints, using Kanban tables, daily stand-up meetings and retrospectives. Parts of the HR function went further and opted for a completely agile organization.

Final assessment: What have we achieved, and
where does Swiss Re stand on the topic of agility today?

Three years after the start of the agile movement and the establishment of the People Circle, it's possible to make a cautious assessment of the results of our efforts and where Swiss Re stands today regarding the topic of agility.

First of all, we can say that the intervention worked. We were able to determine that the organization actually became more agile in the eyes of the employees. Based on our semi-annual pulse surveys, we were able to measure that, after an initial drop in the curve, the adoption of agile behaviors has considerably increased in the eyes of employees. For example, the impression that 'the colleagues with whom I regularly work advocated making decisions at the lowest level of the hierarchy' had risen by 22 percentage points (November 20 compared with May 19).

And the assessment that 'people ask others to take the initiative and make sure something will happen' saw an increase of 10 percentage points (November 20 compared with May 19). The so-called Agility Index (see chart ➜ page 297) also increased significantly from May 2018 to November 2020. This index is created by an external survey provider and measures agile behaviors, e.g. the (perceived) response to customer requests and the speed with which decisions are made. Here Swiss Re developed from ranking slightly below the benchmark of the financial and insurance industry to considerably above the benchmark.

Today, the questions remains whether the Swiss Re approach was actually the best possible one: To start the transformation to more agility as a movement and focus on leadership culture as a connecting element – as compared with a comprehensive agile top-down transformation from the outset. Perhaps the decision to focus initially on leadership culture has actually contributed, as intended, to preparing the organization for a later, complete transformation. At any rate, we can say that the agile transformation is now in full swing; the 'movement' has acquired more structure and more top-down guidance.

Large-scale digital transformation has begun. As part of this transformation, the entire IT area with around 2,000 internal and another 3,000 external employees will be repositioned, with a new operating model and an agile organizational structure in squads, chapters and product areas. The aim is to expand this organizational model to other areas within the group.

> Large-scale digital transformation has begun.

These efforts are supported by a centrally controlled, company-wide training program that aims at improving skill in key technical areas and to boost – that's quite important – cross-functional capabilities such as agile work techniques, data analysis and evaluation as well as digital adoption and advocacy.

In retrospect, it can be said that the development toward a more agile leadership culture has turned out to be enormously helpful in terms of the response to the COVID-19 pandemic. 18 months before the outbreak of the pandemic, the decision for an agile approach (leadership at all levels) had been made and implementation begun.

So the company had just what was needed when the crisis broke in early 2020, when people from everywhere in the organization had to work at home from one day to the next and show 'leadership from every seat.' It should also be noted that the digital transformation and development toward more agility was accelerated by the COVID-19 pandemic at Swiss Re and many, many other enterprises.

Most people have a hard time getting excited about topics they don't understand. **Strategy is no exception.**

Robert Wreschniok

Figure 54: Section of a Big Picture on the growth and internationalization strategy of an organization, TATIN Institute 2023

OUTLOOK

Outlook
The role of leadership in strategy activation

Figure 55:
Who is a 'catalyst leader'
as outlined in School of
Change Management,
TATIN Institute 2023

The Strategy Activation Canvas is for executives of a new generation, a generation of 'catalyst leaders' as Bill Joiner termed it (see mainly Joiner & Josephs 2020 or Hofert 2019). By 'catalyst' (and the stages afterward), Joiner means the role of leaders as coaches, as facilitators, as the people 'who get out of the way' for teams.

This role of leaders is no longer designed hierarchically (not even first among equals); instead, it refers to leadership tasks across the whole team (of decision-making, development of team members, technical and methodological knowledge, etc.). The catalyst is therefore the coach who empowers the other team members in the tasks of leadership; the team is managed jointly (not by one single person).

In most organizations, only a fraction of leaders take on the role of catalyst. It is not the goal to develop all leaders into coaches either – experts and achievers are also needed. However, it's crucial that there be leaders who give decision-making back to the group, especially in cases where decisions should be taken, namely where tensions crop up. To lead teams toward being able to make good decisions on their own.

To assume the role of catalyst, leaders must take a very good look at themselves (to realize and admit honestly what type of leader they are); secondly, they must fight to a certain extent against dominant leadership cultures. Similar to Joiner, the work of Loevinger (see Loevinger 1976) shows that only a fraction of leaders develop personal independence in the first place. Because it's not easy: If I grow up in an environment where 'command and execute' is the dominant idea and I have a career in this environment, this represents a type of leadership whose very foundations I must question.

In addition, I will certainly not gain status through budget management or as a sounder for the people I lead. On the contrary: As a leader, I'm at the service of the teams that develop topics independently; so I'm actually hardly visible at times. The role of leaders in strategy activation derives from these considerations about the role of coach, facilitator. We described this in detail in the introductory chapters: Successfully activated strategies aren't subject to a chain of command and aren't defined from the board to the bottom-most hierarchy level.

On the contrary. Good strategies are understood by everyone, and every individual in the company contributes to the overall good by his work (see above all ❯ Social dynamics that prevent strategy implementation). Teams learn from and inspire one another for how the strategy can work. This means that leaders are moderators, connectors, challengers or visionaries who stimulate new ways of thinking. Leaders are moderators, connectors, challengers or visionaries who stimulate new ways of thinking.

The impact the role of leaders can have has been demonstrated by the consulting firm Gallup, which examined the reasons behind the vigorous growth rates in employee commitment in American companies (cf. Harter 2020). Their conclusion: (1) The development of the corporate culture is up to the CEO and the board. (2) These companies establish a culture of coaches; practice (3) communication that activates the entire company; and (4) they hold their managers accountable.

The exciting thing about it is: The hierarchical 'power' of a leader isn't needed in these companies for propelling topics. Instead, these companies have succeeded in decoupling goal attainment from the role of leadership, so teams and individuals are empowered to create new things.

> Leaders are moderators, connectors, challengers or visionaries who stimulate new ways of thinking.

1

Culture development is a matter for the CEO and the board.

2

These companies establish a culture of coaches, they practice ...

3

... a communication that activates the entire company. And ...

4

... they hold their managers accountable.

Figure 56:
What the role of
leaders can do, in
four dimensions,
according to
Gallup 2020

To allow activation, a leader must let go a little bit (see, above all, the work of Laloux 2016). Leaders turn into people 'who clear the way'; at the same time, they must align teams and departments to a clearly defined guide star. It's called 'aligned autonomy' in the agile world – trusting employees to deal with strategy issues.

Leaders are transformed into facilitators, enablers, challengers and providers of content-related guiding principles. Think of waves: Basically, leaders withdraw from directive work and provide the content-based context for the teams. Functions such as HR, IT, Operations, Communications, etc., then offer the tools required to make the context come alive (e.g. certain capabilities on the part of HR). Employees choose from these tools on their own and use them to bring the current strategy episode to life.

Then it starts again: Refreshed context with different areas of focus or developments from the management team; refreshed tool from the support functions. Etc. The example of ❯ Microsoft: Help shaping a new era – activating Microsoft's strategic core worldwide in this Strategy Activation Canvas impressively demonstrates this interplay: Microsoft established these waves again and again over many years.

Leadership ladder

If you think about the employees you lead – at what 'level' of this ladder would you place them? Do they come to you and say ...

Level 1: 'Tell me what to do'

Level 2: 'I see a problem here' or 'What I would like to know is ...'

Level 3: 'I think we should ...'

Level 4: 'I would like to ...'

Level 5: 'I'll do the following ...'

Level 6: 'I have ...'

Level 7: 'For a long time I have ...'

The seven levels are an indication of how independently your team picks up ideas and issues and pushes them forward without involving you (i.e. level 6 and 7). The levels also show how much you're able to let go and enable your teams to act at levels 6 and 7.

Outlook
And it goes on

The book does not end here. The Strategy Activation Canvas is designed as a handbook, a reference book, as a game manual that enables you to try out new moves over and over, to develop topics further. If you want to go further, you're welcome to share your thoughts, ideas and architectures of strategy activation.

A first point of contact for this is the portal `www.strategy-activation.com`. Here the Canvas is available for download and an opportunity for networking is provided. Are you looking for inspiration on how to activate teams, functions or entire companies? Here you'll find some ideas for tools, templates and the like that help you get started with collaborative formats.

Outlook
Digital tools and platforms
for strategy activation

In the Strategy Activation Canvas, we constantly refer to online tools that support and facilitate the shaping of dialog in major corporations. We compiled the most important tools for you.

Virtual 'boards'

`www.miro.com` A comprehensive virtual whiteboard that can be filled in as you like with virtual sticky notes. With numerous systematic functions for designing the board and analyzing it (e.g. through voting on the virtual sticky notes). Particularly suited for complex workshops or events with many participants.

`www.klaxoon.com` Similar to Miro, not quite as intuitive. Alongside the whiteboard function, Klaxoon provides options of gamification and is therefore particularly suitable for interactive learning formats.

`www.ideaboardz.com` If something has to be done fast: Simple and pragmatic tool to capture ideas quickly and have them evaluated. Ideaboardz cannot do much more, but that's exactly what makes it right for some situations.

Virtual meeting points

`www.wonder.me` Virtual space in which participants communicate with one another through avatars and speech balloons. By getting closer to a discussion group virtually, you can take part in the conversation. Suitable for breakouts, getting to know one another in larger groups, talking about ideas that are presented.

`www.remo.co/guided-tours` is a potential alternative to wonder.me. Remo is an all-in-one platform with broadcast functions, where you can organize live virtual events. They provide a network space and real-time face-to-face engagement.

Virtual collaboration

Something that global corporations have been doing for many years needed to become a feature in many companies on account of the pandemic in the 2020s: Collaboration in virtual environments. What was initially deemed a burden has often-times turned out to be a golden opportunity for interacting easily and directly across sites and national borders. Here are some ideas on how to handle such setups:

`Hales & Grenny (2020)` How to get people to actually participate in virtual meetings. Harvard Business Review. Online: Https://hbr-org.cdn.ampproject.org/c/s/hbr.org/amp/2020/03/how-to-get-people-to-actually-participate-in-virtual-meetings

`biz30.timedoctor.com/virtual-team-building` Good compilation about the topics of team building during virtual offsites, the building of new teams, etc.

Making figures & data visible live

`www.mentimeter.com` To avoid individual opinions at larger events, tools such as Mentimeter offer the opportunity participants about their opinion quickly; all results are then shown live. Whether quantitative or qualitative analyses or the classification into matrices – the options offered are well suited to engage larger groups and engage in a dialog about the results.

`www.ahaslides.com` One example of several alternatives to Mentimeter. Similar in function and easy to operate.

Complete solutions for town-hall meetings or virtual trade fairs

`www.pigeonhole.at` Comprehensive and well-thought-out solution to manage large town-hall meetings interactively. Whether providing an agenda, voting functions (as per Mentimeter), presentation modes or Q&A – Pigeonhole provides a powerful tool for designing traditional town-hall meetings interactively and on a guided basis, available to both participants and administrators.

`www.slido.com` Similar to Pigeonhole; easier operation and less complex. Well suited to the management of town-hall meetings (especially Q&A).

`www.expo-ip.com` With expo-IP, virtual trade fair situations can be created, e.g. on virtual markets. You get support in planning, organization and implementation. The tool offers many additional features, e.g. digital scavenger hunt, gamification, matchmaking, streaming, feedback, training points, live video chat, 3D animation, appointment scheduling, whiteboards, to expand interaction and functionality.

In addition to the tools presented here, there exist countless others – a look into the world of online tools is worth it. Options and applications have developed enormously in recent years; and although you cannot replace live events with them, you can try and compensate for them.

Acceleration platforms

`www.humu.com` Along the lines of 'Connect your teams to drive meaningful impact,' the former HR head of Google developed an acceleration platform with so-called working nudges to stimulate leaders.

`www.day7.io` The acceleration platforms of DAY7 have found an answer to an apparently simple question: How do we take people along on the journey? How can strategy and transformation be communicated successfully so that everyone understands what the destination is and can make a personal contribution to the shared new goals? DAY7 provides an answer by acknowledging that there are different types of people in every company: Those who see and welcome the need for something 'new'; those who are basically willing but have a lot of questions; and those who are opposed to anything new. The DAY7 approach meets all three types by putting the strategic challenge in a broader context and enabling participation from different perspectives.

More

`www.kahoot.com` Interactive learning and gaming tool that is especially suited for the use of game-playing at major events.

`www.oncoo.de` A tool originally intended for schools. It is suitable for mind matching (including random group allocation and timing; or for surveys with the aid of the evaluation target).

Outlook
Author biographies

Adrian Bucher (Kantonalbank Baselland, BLKB) has been head of the Human Resources & Organizational Development of BLKB in Liestal since September 2020. Prior to that he was active as an industrial psychologist and economist for more than 15 years; he held different HR functions at Swisscom; most recently he was responsible for the HR division in the private customer segment of Swisscom. Adi Bucher was one of the agile pioneers at Swisscom. From 2016 to 2018, he was responsible for the issues of leadership, transformation and collaboration, working with Holacracy as an operating system. For several years, he supported the Group management in business transformation. He advocates new work topics as well as a more pronounced purpose orientation. From his point of view, the only constant in our lives is constant change.

Jean-Philippe Courtois (Microsoft) As executive vice president and president of Global Sales, Marketing & Operations, Jean-Philippe Courtois leads Microsoft's commercial business across 124 subsidiaries worldwide. From Cloud services to AI and mixed reality, Courtois is responsible for driving strategic planning, growth initiatives, national digital transformation partnerships and running the Microsoft global commercial business. Courtois is passionate about enabling businesses to transform digitally with the right strategy, skills and technology to ignite new innovation, new ways of working, new business models and new revenue streams.

He helps build vibrant ecosystems with small businesses, start-ups, public sector entities, partners all the way to global industry leaders. Previously, Courtois served as president of Microsoft International where he led sales, marketing and services across all Microsoft subsidiaries outside of the United States and Canada. Before that he held the same role for the EMEA region (Europe, Middle East and Africa) as CEO and president of Microsoft EMEA and was corporate vice president of Worldwide

Customer Marketing, based out of Microsoft's worldwide headquarters in Redmond, Washington. Courtois joined Microsoft in 1984. His first role was as a partner sales representative and, after holding several leadership positions, he was promoted to general manager for Microsoft France in 1994. Courtois holds a Diplôme des Etudes Commerciales Supérieures (DECS) from the Ecole Supérieure de Commerce de Nice (SKEMA).

Outside of Microsoft, Courtois is chairman of the board of directors for SKEMA Business School as well as a board member of Positive Planet, a worldwide leading NGO with a mission to help men and women across the world create the conditions for a better life for future generations. Courtois is also on the board of directors of ManpowerGroup, the global workforce solutions organization. He has served as co-chairman of the World Economic Forum's Global Digital Divide Initiative Task Force, on the European Commission Information and Communication Technology task force and previously sat on the board of directors for AstraZeneca. In 2015, he co-founded the Live for Good foundation, which aims to unlock the potential of young people from all walks of life through social entrepreneurship, driving societal innovation through a purpose-led community.

Barbara Kellerman (Harvard Kennedy School) is the James MacGregor Burns Lecturer in Public Leadership at the Harvard Kennedy School. She is the Founding Executive Director of the School's Center for Public Leadership. Her book 'The End of Leadership' was long listed by the Financial Times as among the Best Business Books and selected by Choice as 'essential' reading. Barbara Kellerman speaks to audiences all over the world. She has served on many different boards and was ranked by Forbes.com as among 'Top 50 Business Thinkers' and by Leadership Excellence in the top 15 of 'thought leaders in management and leadership'.

Beat Knechtli (Baloise) is Swiss and graduated in economics and business administration from Basel University. After working at Hoffmann-La Roche, ABB and PwC, he founded his own company in 2013. In tandem with it, he has been working as organizational developer at Baloise Group since 2013. His focus is on the development and implementation of individual and collective changes of all sorts. As a third pillar, he lectures at various universities and technical colleges in Switzerland. For many years, his ideas and change approaches have been based on this combination of actual practice and theory.

Frank Meyer (E.ON) is CEO at E.ON Italy and former Senior Vice President B2C and E-Mobility Global and Chief Innovation Officer at E.ON SE. Before leading E.ON Italy, he was globally responsible for setting up and accelerating E.ON's innovation and new growth areas such as PV and storage, eMobility, energy management solutions and heat solutions. He was recently selected as one of the top 100 Innovators of Germany by Handelsblatt. In 2012, Mr. Meyer joined Vodafone Germany as Director Strategy and New Business Development, where he was responsible for Corporate Strategy, Innovation, New Business Development and Strategic Programme Management. Among other things, he acted as strategic lead for the Kabel Deutschland acquisition (€10.7 billion acquisition volume).

In the early part of his career he spent from 2006 to 2012 at The Boston Consulting Group. Frank Meyer holds a PhD in Physics from the Max Planck Institute. He majored in Physics and Mathematics at RWTH Aachen, Université Paris Sud, Imperial College London and Ludwig-Maximilians University. Frank is truly international and speaks 7 languages.

Sabine Pundsack (NORD/LB) has been working in various positions at NORD/LB for more than 20 years. She was responsible for various Group projects/programs on a wide variety of topics, e.g. cost optimization, sustainability, major IT projects, and made a name for herself at NORD/LB as a successful turnaround manager.

Since 2019, she has been driving forward a systematic cultural change at the bank along the lines of #zukunftschaffen (creating the future) to activate the NORD/LB 2024 strategy. As the head of HR Controlling (Management Control) & Operations, she is also responsible for the Group-wide HR digitization project SAFiR (launch of SAP SF) and the outsourcing project for the company pension plans.

Oliver Stein (Swisscom) has been working on the link between digital transformation and customer experience for more than 25 years. After getting the German Weather Service on the Internet, he launched Rhein-Main.Net of Frankfurter Allgemeine Zeitung. At Swisscom, he has been working in strategic and operational roles and tasks and has been responsible for customer experience. Always focused on people, he used technical innovations to create new, exciting experiences.

Ulrich Tennie (Swiss Re) joined the Swiss Re Group as Global Head Organisation Development at the firm's headquarters in Zurich in 2018. He has been a driving force in the company's agile transformation, specifically leading on the issues of cultural change, capability building and employee experience. He also supported the turnaround and transformation of the Corporate Solutions business unit. Prior to Swiss Re, Ulrich worked for 12 years for the global healthcare company Novartis where he held Human Resources leadership positions at global, regional and country levels. Ulrich has a background in strategy and HR consulting with Monitor Deloitte and Towers Perrin (now Willis Towers Watson) respectively, having been based in the firms' Frankfurt, London and New York offices. He holds a Bachelor degree in Business Management from ESB Business School (Reutlingen/London) and a Masters degree in Industrial Relations from London School of Economics.

Dr. Ansgar Thiessen (Swiss Re), Global Head Operational Excellence, is a member of the Operations Management Committee at Swiss Re Corporate Solutions and a founding member of the so-called Strategy Activation Group. Prior to that, he spent many years in leadership positions in change management consultancies. For more than ten years, he has been a thought leader in how organizations can make their strategies acceptable and powerful. Today, Mr. Thiessen is a regular lecturer and author on the subject at international business schools such as CBS Copenhagen or IMD Lausanne.

Tony White (Allianz) is the former Global Head of Allianz University (AllianzU), a position he has held since July 2017. He joined Allianz SE in November 2016 as the Head of the Group People Development team prior to appointment to his current role. He is responsible for the implementation and setup of the new Allianz University (AllianzU) to support the Global Learning and Leadership Development programs and systems. Prior to joining the Allianz SE, he worked for Allianz Global Investors as the Head of L&D and Talent management for Europe, which he joined from Coca Cola Enterprises. In this role, he was responsible for the implementation of a Learning Management System, introducing new and innovative approaches to learning for the business and development of the social recruitment aspect in the talent management process. He performed the role of the Head of Talent management (globally), which involved leading the annual talent management process, graduate recruitment, Annual Engagement Survey and the AllianzGI end-of-year people processes.

He holds a diploma in Electronic Engineering and is a graduate of Sheffield University, where he received his Master's Degree in Education, Training and Development. Tony is also a Fellow of the Irish Institute of Training and Development (FIITD).

Kaja Wilkniss (HCOB) manages the HR strategy at Hamburg Commercial Bank (HCOB) and has accompanied the transformation of the bank after change of ownership from the very beginning as the person responsible for the 'change' workstream that she has initiated together with her team. 15 years of experience in the crisis-ridden banking environment had a formative influence on her. She has held many roles in HR development, HR management and HR strategy. She stands for the new generation of leadership and describes herself as demanding and bothersome, at the same time as an absolute team player with a focus on people, without losing her sense of humor and fun.

Robert Wreschniok (TATIN) is the CEO of the TATIN Institute for Strategy Activation with offices in Munich, Basel, Hong Kong and Zurich. For more than 20 years, he has supported organizations in strategy activation and acceleration of transformation processes. He is a board member of the Cluster for Innovation and Digital Transformation (CIDT). And a member of the Design Strategy Board, Basel, since 2015.

Robert Wreschniok is a lecturer who is much in demand as well as the author of numerous publications, e.g. 'Strategie-Aktivierung: Wie abstrakte Konzepte wirksam werden' (2019), 'Der ganz normale Change Wahnsinn' (2016),' 'Reputation Capital: Building and Maintaining Trust in the 21st Century' (2009) and 'Strategisches Management von Mergers & Acquisitions' (2006).

Outlook
Studies and academic literature cited

- Anand, Bharat N. & Barsoux, Jean-Louis (2017): What everyone gets wrong about change management. Harvard Business Review November-December. Online at https://hbr.org/2017/11/what-everyone-gets-wrong-about-change-management

- Bradley, Chris; Hirt, Martin & Smit, Sven (2018): Strategy Beyond the Hockey Stick. People, Probabilities and Big Moves to Beat the Odds. Wiley.

- Buckingham, Marcus & Goodall, Ashley: Nine Lies about Work. A Freethinking Leaders Guide to the Real World. Ingram Publisher Services.

- Covey, Steve (1989): The Seven Habits of Highly Effective People. Simon & Schuster.

- Choudhury, Prithwiraj (2020): Our Work-from-Anywhere Future. Online at: Https://hbr.org/2020/11/our-work-from-anywhere-future

- Clifford, Catherine (2020): Jeff Bezos to exec after product totally flopped: 'You can't, for one minute, feel bad'. Online at: Https://www.cnbc.com/2020/05/22/jeff-bezos-why-you-cant-feel-bad-about-failure.html

- Deloitte Development LLC. Member of Deloitte ToucheTohmatsu Limited (2014) Online at: Https://www2.deloitte.com/content/dam/Deloitte/global/Documents/HumanCapital/gx-cons-hc-learning-solutions-placemat.pdf

- Detert, J. & Trevino, L. (2010): Speaking up to higher-ups: How supervisors and skip-level leader influence employee voice. Organization Science, 21(1), 249–270.

- Dignan, Aaron (2019): Brave New Work – Are You Ready to Reinvent Your Organization? Portfolio Penguin.

- Edmondson, A. & Zhike, L. (2014):Psychological Safety: The History, Renaissance, and Future of an Interpersonal Construct. Annual Review of Organizational Psychology and Organizational Behavior. Vol. 1:23-43 (Volume publication date March 2014).

- Eppler, Martin & Kernbach, Sebastian (2018): Meet Up!
  Einfach bessere Besprechungen durch Nudging. Ein Impulsbuch für Leiter,
  Moderatoren und Teilnehmer von Sitzungen. Schäffer-Poeschel.

- Ewenstein, Boris, Smith, Wesley, & Sologar, Ashvin (2015): Changing change
  management. McKinsey Digital. Online at: Https://www.mckinsey.com/
  featured-insights/leadership/changing-change-management

- Fischer, Isolde & Wetzel, Ralf (2015): Die Macht der Improvisation.
  Zeitschrift für Organisationsentwicklung, Heft 4.

- Friedman, R. (2021): 5 Things High-Performing Teams Do Differently.
  Hint: It's not always about the work. Online at: Https://hbr.org/2021/10/5-
  things-high-performing-teams-do-differently

- Christina Fritsch (Forbes) 'How to Foster Psychological Safety in Your Team'.

- Gioia, Stephanie (2016): Nine pitfalls of strategy activation.
  Online at: Https://xplane.com/nine-pitfalls-of-strategy-activation/

- Glaveski, Steve (2020): The five levels of remote work – and why you're
  probably at level 2. Online at: Https://medium.com/swlh/the-five-levels-
  of-remote-work-and-why-youre-probably-at-level-2-ccaf05a25b9c

- Goller, I. & Laufer, T. (2018): Psychologische Sicherheit in Unternehmen.
  Wie Hochleistungsteams wirklich funktionieren. Springer.

- Harter, Jim (2020): 4 factors driving record-high employee engagement in U.S.
  Online at: Https://www.gallup.com/workplace/284180/factors-driving-
  record-high-employee-engagement.aspx

- Heath, Chip & Heath, Dan (2017): The Power of Movements.
  Why Certain Experiences Have Extraordinary Impact. Simon & Schuster.

- Hofert, Svenja (2019): 5 levels of leadership agility – und warum das nächste Level eine Krise braucht. Online at: Https://teamworks-gmbh.de/5-levels-of-leadership-agility-und-warum-das-naechste-level-eine-krise-braucht/

- Joiner, William B. & Josephs, Stephen A. (2006): Leadership Agility. Five Levels of Mastery For Anticipating and Initiating Change. Wiley.

- Kahnemann, Daniel (2012): Thinking Fast and Slow. Penguin.

- Kellerman, Barbara (2016): Leadership – it's a system, not a person! Daedalus. Vol. 145, Issue 3, Pages 83-94. MIT Press Journals.

- Kellerman, Barbara (2012): The End of Leadership. HarperCollins.

- Kellerman, Barbara (2008): Followership: How Followers are Creating Change and Changing Leaders. Harvard Business School Press.

- Kim, W. Chan & Mauborgne, Renée (2005): Blue Ocean Strategy. How to Create Uncontested Market Space and Make the Competition Irrelevant. Harvard Business School Press.

- Kotter, John P. (2007): Leading Change: Why Transformation Efforts Fail. Harvard Business Review. Online at: Https://hbr.org/2007/01/leading-change-why-transformation-efforts-fail

- Kotter, John P. (2018): The 8-step process for leading change. Online at: Https://www.kotterinc.com/8-steps-process-for-leading-change/

- Laloux, Frederic (2016): Reinventing Organisations. Ein illustrierter Leitfaden sinnstiftender Formen der Zusammenarbeit. Vahlen.

- Largo, Remo (2017): Das passende Leben. Fischer Taschenbuch.

- Lewin, Kurt (1947): Frontiers in group dynamics. Concept, method and reality in social science. Social equilibria and social change. In: Human Relations. Vol. 1, no. 1.

- Loevinger, Jane (1976): Ego Development. Conceptions and Theories. Jossey-Bass, San Francisco.

- Marquet, David (2013): Greatness. Online at https://www.youtube.com/watch?v=OqmdLcyES_Q

- Mohr, Niko., Woehe, Jens & Diebold, Marcus (1998): Widerstand erfolgreich managen. Professionelle Kommunikation in Veränderungsprojekten. Frankfurt/Main: Campus Verlag.

- Osterwalder, Alexander & Pigneur, Yves (2011). Business Model Generation. Ein Handbuch für Visionäre, Spielveränderer und Herausforderer. Campus.

- anon. (2021): Statista Research (2021): Size of the global consulting market from 2011 to 2020. Online at: Https://www.statista.com/statistics/466460/global-management-consulting-market-size-by-sector/

- anon. (2019) Strategy Activation. Accelerate strategy execution and harness the collective ingenuity of teams. Online at: Http://ey-box.com/wp-content/uploads/2019/12/2-Activating-new-strategies.pdf

- anon. (2019): EyBox – Strategy Activation Accelerate strategy execution and harness the collective ingenuity of teams. Online at: Http://ey-box.com/wp-content/uploads/2019/12/2-Activating-new-strategies.pdf

- anon. (2018): School for Change Agents – The Change Agent of the Future. Online at: Https://www.slideshare.net/HorizonsCIC/school-for-change-agents-2018-the-change-agent-of-the-future

- anon. (2018): Market Study Bundesverband Deutscher Unternehmensberater BDU e.V. – Fact & Figures zum Beratermarkt 2018. Online at: Https://www.bdu.de/newsletter/ausgabe-22018/facts-figures-zum-beratermarkt-consultants-weiter-im-hoehenflug/

- anon. (2017): State of the global workplace. Online at: Https://www.gallup.com/workplace/238079/state-global-workplace-2017.aspx

- anon. (2015): Hays, HR-Report 2015/2016.
  Online at: HR Report 2021 – New Work | Hays.

- anon. (n.d.): Consulting Industry Global.
  Online at: Https://www.consultancy.org/consulting-industry/global

- anon. (n.d.): Organisational Culture: Beyond Employee Engagement – Whitepaper.
  Online at: Https://www.human-synergistics.com.au/docs/default-source/de-fault-document-library/organisational-culture---beyond-employee-engagement

- Repucci, Sarah (n.d.): A leaderless struggle for democracy. Online at: https://freedomhouse.org/report/freedom-world/2020/leaderless-struggle-democracy

- Sachs, Jonah (2012): Winning the Story Wars. Why those who tell – and live – the best stories will rule the future. Harvard Business Review Press.

- Scharmer, Otti & Kaufer, Katrin (2013): Leading From the Emerging Future. From Ego-system to Eco-system Economies. Berrett-Koehler Publishers.

- Schultz, Howard (2011): Onward. How Starbucks Fought for Its Life Without Losing its Soul. Wiley.

- Sull, Donald, Sull, Charles & Yoder, James (2018): No One Knows Your Strategy — Not Even Your Top Leaders. Online at: Https://sloanreview.mit.edu/article/no-one-knows-your-strategy-not-even-your-top-leaders/

- Tan, Chade-Meng (2012): Seach inside yourself. Chade-Meng Tan talks at Google. Online at: Https://www.youtube.com/watch?v=r8fcqrNO7so

- Techt, Uwe (2010): Goldratt und die Theory of Constraints: Der Quantensprung im Management.

- Thesmann, Stephan (2016): Menschliche Informationsverarbeitung. Springer Fachmedien.

- Thiessen, Ansgar & Wreschniok, Robert: Strategy Activation. Wie abstrakte Konzepte wirksam werden. Zeitschrift für Organisationsentwicklung. No. 3/2019 (p. 63-68).

- Velazco, Chris (2018): Amazon's flop phone made newer, better hardware possible. Online at: Https://www.engadget.com/2018-01-13-amazon-s-flop-of-a-phone-made-newer-better-hardware-possible.html

- Wilson, Marianne (2020): Challenger, Gray & Christmas. CEO turnover in 2019 was 'staggering'. Chain Store Age. Online at: Https://chainstoreage.com/challenger-gray-christmas-ceo-turnover-2019-was-staggering

- Zook, Chris & Allen, James (2010): Profit from the core. A return to growth in turbulent times. Harvard Business Review Press.

Footnotes

1. The derivation was first published in Zeitschrift für Organisationsentwicklung (Journal for Organizational Development) no. 3, 2019: 'Strategie-Aktivierung. Wie abstrakte Konzepte wirksam werden'.

2. Quantitative analysis of 2,393 companies from the data set of McKinsey Corporate Performance Analytics. Data analyzed over a period of 5 years (2000-2004; 2005-2009; 2010-2014) The data set includes 59 industries from 62 countries.

3. In 2015-2016, 532 decision-makers, of which 49 percent came from Germany, 20 percent from Austria and 32 percent from Switzerland, took part in the online survey on the HR Report.

4. Based on data of 4,012 study participants from 124 companies, with comparatively high response rates at all investigated hierarchy levels. The data was collected between 2012 and 2017.

5. This text was first published in Zeitschrift für Organisationsentwicklung (Journal for Organizational Development) no. 3, 2019: 'Strategie-Aktivierung. Wie abstrakte Konzepte wirksam werden'.

6. This text was first published in Zeitschrift für Organisationsentwicklung (Journal for Organizational Development) no. 3, 2019: 'Strategie-Aktivierung. Wie abstrakte Konzepte wirksam werden'.

References, Swiss Re

- Aghina W., Handscomb C., Salo O, Thaker S. (2021), 'The Impact of Agility: How to Shape Your Organization to Compete,' McKinsey Quarterly

- Behrens P. (2018), 'Agile Leadership,' Handbook used to support executive leadership training at Swiss Re in November 2018, ScrumAlliance

- Brosseau D., Ebrahim S., Handscomb C., Thaker S. (2019), 'The Journey to An Agile Organization', McKinsey Quarterly

- Denning S. (2018), 'The Age of Agile,' American Management Association

- Rigby D., Elk S. and Berez S. (2020), 'Doing Agile Right,' Harvard Business Review Press

- Schlüter J. (2020), 'Leadership from Every Seat', Swiss Re case study in Shaping the Future of Transformational Learning edited by Roland Deiser, ECLF Press

- Snowden D.J. and Boone M.E. (2007), 'A leader's framework for decision making', Harvard Business Review